Trust Their Struggle

Trust Their Struggle

A Christian Approach to Proactive Suicide Prevention in Children and Youth for Parents, Pastors, and the Christian Community

Arielle Bazulka

WIPF & STOCK · Eugene, Oregon

TRUST THEIR STRUGGLE
A Christian Approach to Proactive Suicide Prevention in Children and Youth for Parents, Pastors, and the Christian Community

Copyright © 2025 Arielle Bazulka. All rights reserved. Except for brief quotations in critical publications or reviews, no part of this book may be reproduced in any manner without prior written permission from the publisher. Write: Permissions, Wipf and Stock Publishers, 199 W. 8th Ave., Suite 3, Eugene, OR 97401.

Wipf & Stock
An Imprint of Wipf and Stock Publishers
199 W. 8th Ave., Suite 3
Eugene, OR 97401

www.wipfandstock.com

PAPERBACK ISBN: 979-8-3852-3087-7
HARDCOVER ISBN: 979-8-3852-3088-4
EBOOK ISBN: 979-8-3852-3089-1

VERSION NUMBER 01/29/25

Scriptures taken from the Holy Bible, New International Version®, NIV®. Copyright © 1973, 1978, 1984, 2011 by Biblica, Inc.™ Used by permission of Zondervan. All rights reserved worldwide. www.zondervan.com The "NIV" and "New International Version" are trademarks registered in the United States Patent and Trademark Office by Biblica, Inc.™

Contents

Preface: Chaplain Testimony—Changing the Book | vii
Acknowledgement | ix

1 A Community Investment | 1
2 Developmental Considerations | 8
3 Cultural Considerations and World Application | 22
4 Case Studies | 42
5 Practical Exercise Workbook | 59

Bibliography | 167

Preface
Chaplain Testimony—Changing the Book

SITTING IN MY OFFICE, staring at a white wall for what seemed like hours, unable to move, I recounted every second of those days, hours, and minutes leading up to the meeting I had to sit through today. One of my girls, my students, died by suicide last night. She was thirteen. She came from a wealthy family. She had brown hair, brown eyes, loved the violin, and played soccer. And she came to me a month ago asking for help, and I followed the book. My responsibility as a youth pastor was to tell the parents. Let them know their daughter was depressed and wanted help. That was all my job description entailed, and that was all I did. Now, as I waited for my youth group to arrive, as I planned a new program for the evening that would involve a vigil set out for a young girl I let down, I thought, the book needs to change.

This was not my first encounter with suicide, but it was the first time I was in the lineup of adults that a child had reached out to for help and ultimately failed to provide. Suicide has played a large role in my life. Having grown up an Army brat, many of my family members and friends have attempted to take their own lives over the years for one reason or another. As a child myself, I was diagnosed with general anxiety disorder, but my parents fell into the same pattern as other parents of the time; with lines of questioning that held "what do you have to be stressed about". It wasn't that I was unloved; on the contrary, I grew up in a loud and loving home that was full of life. This was just the mentality surrounding mental illness for my

Preface

generation. I would become so stressed out at times that I would lose chunks of my hair or black out from an anxiety attack or suffer from migraines that could last for days. I remember as a youth I threw myself into the church, believing that God would pull me back from what I called my darkness. In a lot of ways, I was right. I could feel Jesus when I sat in church and laid my head on the pew, hoping for a reprieve. I could feel him when I sat in my room at night, reading my Bible and looking for the comfort of the divine. I taught myself breathing techniques and meditation practices, and I prayed . . . a lot. At the age of 14 I would attempt to take my life for the first time. My saving grace would be my lack of education on what pills specifically can kill you. As I attempted to swallow as many Tylenol extra-strength medication as I could, eventually, my stomach would give out, and instead of dying, I spent the night sleeping over the toilet praying the pain in my stomach would end. I wouldn't ultimately have access to therapy until after my second attempt, when I was twenty-two years old, by the insistence of my husband to get help so I would live long enough to be a part of our sons' lives.

By the time I lost my youth group student to suicide, I was well acquainted with the issues in the system regarding youth receiving the care they need in an adequate time frame to combat suicide. That night, after the vigil with our youth group and the offer extended to provide a listening ear to any student who wanted it, I sat down and began my research. Within two weeks I had a general proposal ready to present to my church leadership on a new program, and within a month, I was actively teaching our youth group breathing techniques and some self-care techniques at the start of every meeting.

My program eventually grew. What started as a ten-to-twenty-minute exercise at the start of our youth group meetings would grow over the course of ten years into a non-profit organization with a sixteen-week curriculum that guides youth through spiritual self-care, emotional regulation, and education on mental illness. My only goal is to provide a better "by the book" standard for our churches and families to follow that addresses the problem and doesn't pass the puck to someone else. I failed someone once. I won't make the same mistake twice.

Acknowledgements

THANK YOU TO DR. Jim Lawrence who encouraged me to seek publishing after I graduated from my doctorate program and helped me to determine which publishers to apply to. Thank you to Kris Cameron who helped me through my own struggles. Thank you to my friends and family who support me in my life journey. None of this would have been possible without the love and support of those around me.

1

A Community Investment

"For I know the plans I have for you," declares the LORD, "plans to prosper you and not to harm you, plans to give you hope and a future.

—JER 29:11

THIS BOOK WAS CREATED as a proactive solution toward helping children and youth learn social-emotional skills and resilience skills before the development of anxiety and depression. This book is for the community to become part of the solution in their children's overall development. This book is for parents, pastors, and Christian community leaders who want to be part of the solution.

Youth suicide is a complex issue with various causes and risk factors that can be completely dependent on either genetic identity or social identity conditional on each individual youth. Suicide is defined as "a fatal self-injurious act with some evidence of intent to die."[1] Suicide among youth is the second leading cause of death among children between the ages of nine and sixteen years old within the United States, following directly behind vehicle-related deaths. Statistics show that there is one death due to suicide every

1. Turecki and Brent, "Suicide and Suicidal Behaviour," 1228.

twenty seconds worldwide, or 10.7 individuals for every 100 individuals will take their own life.[2] The risk of suicidal ideation increases rapidly at age twelve years. The consistently rising statistics of suicide among youth should be considered a serious health epidemic when we reflect on the secondary costs to communities and social consequences. The most staggering statistic addresses the reality that the majority of youth who attempt suicide for the first time were undiagnosed with a mental illness. This suggests that the programs we currently have are only effective if a person has been identified as suffering from anxiety or depression. This is an unaddressed gap in the current plan of action to combat suicide across developed countries.

Suicide is predicated by thoughts of death and self-hatred. This phenomenon is defined as suicidal ideation. Psychological factors and personality differences such as hopelessness, impulsivity, and resilience all have a bearing on a person's likelihood of experiencing suicidal ideation.[3] There are several theories developed regarding the cause of suicidal ideation including Bronfenbrenner's ecological system theory. This theory was developed in 2010 and is one of the most recent theoretical models available. This model suggests that social phenomena develop through the interaction of the individual with their environment; this idea has been applied to classify risk factors for suicide.[4] In more recent year's research has turned to the biopsychosocial context in which suicidal ideation can influence behavioral patterns in youth. The most well-known is the Integrated Motivational Volitional (IMV) model of suicidal behavior. This model focuses on factors contributing to suicidal ideation development and the factors that might influence its development into suicidal behavior.[5]

Suicidal behavior is when an individual exhibits signs of self-harm or destructive behavior without committing the act of suicide. Another term utilized for this phenomenon is called

2. "Preventing Suicide," 25–27.
3. O'Connor and Nock, "Psychology of Suicidal Behaviour."
4. Lee et al., "Ecological Understanding of Youth Suicide."
5. Arnautovska and Grad, "Attitudes Toward Suicide."

A Community Investment

alexithymia. The precise definition of alexithymia changes depending on the expert, but the general idea behind this term is the dissociation between feelings and the ability to verbally express those feelings.[6] Alexithymia is considered one of the primary correspondences when correlating developmental deficiencies "as a life-long dispositional factor that can lead to psychosomatic illness."[7] A systematic questionnaire titled the Toronto Alexithymia Scale (TAS) was developed in order to accurately diagnose the correlation between difficulty identifying and distinguishing between feelings and bodily sensations, the ability to put feelings into words and verbalize them to others, and external-orientated thinking.[8] The correlation between alexithymia and suicide in youth has not been studied extensively. However, the correlation of alexithymia and self-harm, combined with the correlation of self-harm and suicidal behavior, cannot be ignored.

The desire to develop new behavioral models and adapt to social norms in order to find their place in the culture, all while battling sexual maturity, can be difficult for any adolescent. The American Psychological Association's annual "Stress in America" report found that 91 percent of Generation Z has experienced physical and sociological symptoms associated with chronic stress.[9] It is important to show how stressors on youth can have a significant contributing factor to suicidal ideation. Stress is the biological response to overly demanding situations. Chronic stress is when the body is placed in a stress state for an extended period of time. Common causes of this are high-pressure academic expectations, peer victimization, and challenging relationships. Chronic stress has been linked in various studies to the development of mental health illnesses such as adjustment disorder, anxiety, depression, and suicidal ideation.

"Adjustment disorder (AjD) is recognized as a stress-response syndrome, which is defined as a maladaptive reaction to

6. Brewer et al., "Alexithymia."
7. Goerlich, "Multifaceted Nature of Alexithymia," 9.
8. Goerlich, "Multifaceted Nature of Alexithymia," 5
9. "Stress in America," 4.

Trust Their Struggle

an identifiable stressor."[10] Adjustment disorders are situationally specific to the individual. Individuals who experience this mental health disorder will often exhibit signs of risk-taking and destructive behavior. Adjustment disorders are associated with impulsive behavior, self-destruction, and suicidal ideation. These disorders are linked to trauma, and stress-related disorders and are usually diagnosed when a person reacts irrationally to an event, but the reaction is not long-term.[11]

Anxiety disorders are defined by the American Psychological Association (APA) as "an emotion characterized by feelings of tension, worried thoughts and physical changes like increased blood pressure."[12] Everyday anxiety is normal for most individuals. An anxiety disorder is characterized by an irrational reaction to the triggering event. The individual experiencing anxiety may experience moments of nausea or have suddenly high blood pressure. Other symptoms can include restlessness, insomnia, increased irritability, and panic attacks.

Depression is defined by the Mayo Clinic as "a mood disorder that causes a persistent feeling of sadness and loss of interest."[13] Symptoms in teens and adolescents can differ from those in an adult. These symptoms may include sadness, irritability, feeling negative and worthless, anger, poor performance or poor attendance at school, feeling misunderstood and extremely sensitive, using recreational drugs or alcohol, eating, or sleeping too much, self-harm, loss of interest in normal activities, and avoidance of social interaction.

The development of stress as the origin for depression can be the result of multiple converging factors. Negative mental health has been commonly connected to stress and anxiety. Prior to receiving treatment for mental illness, most patients will experience chronic stressors, which lead to behavioral changes such as guilt, shame, and depression. These are all beginning symptoms of

10. O'Donnell et al., "Adjustment Disorder," 1–2.
11. O'Donnell et al., "Adjustment Disorder," 4.
12. American Psychological Association, "Anxiety."
13. "Depression" (Mayo Clinic).

A Community Investment

mental illness, and understanding the connection between stress and mental illness is important in understanding the "why?" in youth suicidal ideation. Living with a mental illness can be confusing for an adolescent. Adolescents will often demonstrate detachment from friends and family and might possibly experience panic attacks, unreasonable fear, lack of appetite, or excess appetite. They may also experience moments of depression and possible insomnia. Stressors in life cause stressors on the body.

In general, most experts agree that the cause of suicide in youth is an extremely complex question that warrants extensive study, per region and demographic. While among all current studies the variation of causes studied and the correlation between biopsychosocial influences differ vastly in explanations and emphasis, there are similarities that continuously present themselves. The youth's individual environment is primarily considered to contribute to the risk factor in suicidal ideation. There is significant evidence indicating that three areas of connectedness for youth significantly decrease their risk factor for suicidal ideation and depression. The three areas are family, non-institutional, and institution. Each of these three levels of connectedness has a benefit that can be a turning point for at risk youth. In family connectedness, youth who reported having a positive relationship with their parents also reported lower levels of depression and suicidal ideation. Non-institutional relationships would include friend groups. Youth that have an unstructured friend group that allows for self-discovery have been associated with lower risk rates of suicidal ideation. Youth who reported victimization or bullying and low connectedness to school reported higher levels of depression and suicidal ideation. Religious institutions are another institutional connection that has demonstrated positive effects on youth through healthy attitudes, behaviors, and psychological outcomes. Researchers have found that religious affiliation, importance of religion, and frequency of attendance at respective religious institutions are positively associated with youths' overall psychological health.[14] Loss of connectedness in any of the three areas of social

14. Cole-Lewis et al., "Protective Role of Religious Involvement."

identity for youth can contribute to risk factors in suicidal ideation and suicidal actions.

There are many possible reasons why suicide among youth has been rising over the last two decades. Various studies that included interviews with youth have cited educational standards and bullying among social groups as the two primary stressor concerns. The correlation between educational demands and the rise in suicidal ideation, combined with social expectations, is believed to be among them. Academic stress in adolescents is common, and many students have been told that academic success is the only way to be a successful adult. Many students will prioritize school over emotional and physical health in order to achieve their academic goals. This strategy can cause long-term emotional and mental health problems for adolescents.

The first Latin Grammar school was established in 1635 by the Puritans, and the curriculum consisted primarily of the study of Latin and Greek Literature, as well as religious denominationalism. These schools focused lessons on reading, writing, and arithmetic. The student's overall performance throughout their education was used as an entrance test into Harvard College. Since the inception of education into the standard societal norms of the United States, both positive and negative evolutions have come out of the progress of education. Moving forward into the 1900s, the education system became streamlined in standardized testing and increased emphasis on mathematics and scientific studies. By the latter part of the twentieth century, the United States had developed a desire to become the leading power in mathematics and science education. This perspective leads to consequences put on the educators and administrators if their students did not perform well on state-run standardized testing. As a result, over the next few decades, schools would begin to require more advanced knowledge of their students at earlier ages. Consequences were also established on the youth who could not maintain academic achievements to the expected standards of the state. The resulting pressure on the youth has led to rising stress rates among the demographic that have exceeded the stress rates of adults. Youth

A Community Investment

reported to "Stress in America" an average of a 5.8 stress level on a 10-point scale, versus 5.1 for adults. This rate is significantly higher than what is believed to be a healthy range for the eleven to sixteen age group (3.9).[15]

Peer victimization, or bullying, is the experience of being a target of aggressive behavior from peers of similar age. A study done by Dorothy L. Espelage, a PhD in educational philosophy, found that "peer victimization was found to be related to both suicidal ideation (odds ratio, 2.23 [95% CI, 2.10–12.37]) and suicide attempts (2.55 [1.95–93.34]) among children and adolescents."[16] According to the Center for Disease Control (CDC), approximately 20 percent of students between eleven and sixteen years old have experienced bullying. Alarmingly, approximately 30 percent of youth in the same age bracket admitted to bullying others.[17] Over the years peer victimization has become more prevalent among social norms. Peer victimization can refer to peer to peer, group to peer, group to group, and cyber bullying. The purpose of bullying is to generate a foundation of fear in the victim. The mental and emotional damage that peer victimization can have on adolescents has been shown to elicit similar brain activity and emotional responses as soldiers who are experiencing post-traumatic stress disorder (PTSD).[18] Over the years peer victimization has progressed into the cyber-world. This disconnect from reality has made peer victimization easier, with fewer emotional or physical consequences to the perpetrator.

While the task of identifying specific youth with suicidal ideation would take organized consistent mental health evaluations of each individual youth worldwide, a more pragmatic approach to combating suicidal ideation and behavior is to proactively include resilience education in early childhood education.

---

15. "American Psychological Association Survey," 1.

16. Gini and Espelage, "Peer Victimization, Cyberbullying, and Suicide Risk," 545

17. Kim et al., "Cyberbullying and Victimization and Youth Suicide Risk," 251–57.

18. Sharp, "How Much Does Bullying Hurt," 81–88.

2
Developmental Considerations

"For this very reason, make every effort to supplement your faith with virtue, and virtue with knowledge, and knowledge with self-control, and self-control with steadfastness, and steadfastness with godliness, and godliness with brotherly affection, and brotherly affection with love. For if these qualities are yours and are increasing, they keep you from being ineffective or unfruitful in the knowledge of our Lord Jesus Christ."
—2 PET 1:5–8

FAITH DEVELOPMENT AND SPIRITUAL development are two completely different terms often incorrectly utilized interchangeably. Faith development invokes the development of a specific belief such as understanding the belief in Jesus or in another deity by a religious organization, whereas spiritual development focuses on personal reflection of the transcendental and metaphysical. Spiritual growth is relevant specifically to reflective thoughts and concerns surrounding the meaning of one's life and our overall existence. A person's spirituality can be broken down into three separate categories: a person's moral aims, moral self-judgments,

Developmental Considerations

and metaphysical vision.[1] Moral aims include those positive goals pursued daily and can include aspects such as wanting to be a better person by donating time to a homeless shelter. Moral self-judgments are opinions that an individual forms about themselves based on their experiences while pursuing their moral aims. Metaphysical vision translates to an individual's understanding of how their reality works.

Often this journey utilizes beliefs, practices, and rituals to motivate growth. Spiritual growth can include specific religions, but a person can be spiritual and not religious. The spiritual development's orientation toward ultimate meaning makes it a hermeneutic phenomenon because it involves interpreting life through an ultimate meaning-making framework.[2]

Spiritual growth in adolescents must be fostered through the leaders and influencers in their lives. Spiritual growth is more about fostering specific conditions that allow that growth to occur. These conditions are necessary to ensure that the adolescent is receiving adequate guidance. In general, most theologians and philosophers break down the conditions into seven or eight categories.

It starts with an understanding of the age group and what is appropriate with age and growth in thinking, personality, and judgment skills. In laments terminology, it is essential that the facilitator accepts their development as appropriate for their mental age. An example might be a five-year-old that interprets the world revolving around their existence. This would be a normal response for a child this age and should not be discouraged or encouraged but acknowledged as normal growth.

Participation in organizational activities that have deeper meanings but are age-appropriate for understanding and involvement. These roles should be meaningful to the adolescent and recognizable as a pivotal role to the community. This level of involvement in their organization fosters a feeling of acceptance and trust toward the adolescent and encourages continued positive participation in spiritual growth.

1. Lasair, "What's the Point."
2. Lasair, "What's the Point."

Next, intergenerational involvement between the youth and the older demographic within the community provides an opportunity for guidance and growth, not just for the adolescents but for the older demographic as well. These activities combine an element of the old and the new coming together to form bonds and trust. This fosters an environment where continuous growth and learning are encouraged.

Trust, security, and empathic human understanding combine to foster a mindset for spiritual growth. This is where the family of the adolescents comes into play. In psychology, it has been determined that in order for an adolescent to become a well-rounded adult they require three points of contact while children. One of those points of contact must be within the home environment. By encouraging family interactions within the organization, a level of trust, security, and empathic human understanding can develop and flood over into the home environment. By giving the youth a point of contact for the home through the community, two points of contact are established. Spiritual development relies heavily on personal development. Therefore, involvement of the institution in the family life of the adolescent inspires proper spiritual growth.

Spirituality is an individual journey that encompasses a person's life experiences, individual personality, moral development, and how a person interprets their own spirituality. It is often linked to faith development but not always. In order for a community or organization to engage in spiritual development, they need to understand the individuality of the process itself and respect each individual's journey.

Support systems must be present in the lives of the adolescent for periods of difficulty or crisis, personal despair, or transitions. During these times, faith development may stall, and personal beliefs may be tested or reconsidered. In order to foster a positive environment for spiritual development, the community must foster an environment of support. This may look like having a counselor on staff who can guide individuals through their thoughts and feelings. Peer-to-peer counseling groups are another way to foster this support system.

Developmental Considerations

Finally, there needs to be a willingness to engage the adolescents constructively in questioning and exploring more deeply the fundamental beliefs that are socialized by parents and others in the community. This needs to be done without inspiring fear of rejection, denigration, or expulsion.[3] Spiritual development is characterized by the soul of an individual growing beyond their existential existence and learning to self-regulate and grow within their faith, their mind, and their personality.

Faith is the interpretation of the way a person experiences their life from birth until the day of transition. Our faith development is directly tied to how we perceive our actions, beliefs, and emotional responses or moral development. Faith development theory was developed as a means of determining how the conceptualization of God during childhood has a direct effect on our evolution of core values and beliefs. These core pieces of the human psyche help in understanding an individual's choices in personal relationships, including an individual's relationship to themselves. The formative and developmental relationship between faith development and emotional development creates a need for a dissection into this subject in order to articulate why pastoral counselors have relevancy in suicide prevention.

There are four general characterizations of positive faith development. Faith must "give coherence and direction to persons' lives, link them in shared trusts and loyalties with others, ground their personal stances and communal loyalties in a sense of relatedness to a larger frame of reference, and enable them to face and deal with the challenges of human life and death, relying on that which has the quality of ultimacy in their lives."[4]

We will explore faith development theory alongside moral development theory from the time of infancy until the age of adolescents. The stages of faith development theory determined by Fowler are the most widely accepted and are typically broken down into Primal Faith, Intuitive-Projective Faith, Mythic-Literal Faith,

---

3. Nastasi, *International Handbook*, 65–80.
4. Roehikepartain et al., *Handbook of Spiritual Development*, 97.

and Synthetic-Conventional Faith.[5] Each stage of development affects the outcome of the next developmental stage in a child's growth. The stages of moral development theory determined by Kohlberg are widely accepted and are broken down into six different stages. These include obedience and punishment orientation, individualism and exchange, good interpersonal relationships, maintaining social order, social contract and individual rights, and universal principles. Moral development is often growth in conjunction with faith development.

In the following descriptions of the stages, there is acknowledgment to the realization that all children develop differently and at different paces. The time frames assigned to each stage is a generalization utilized based on the neurotypical child and does not account for children on the neurodivergent spectrum. Development in faith involves biological maturation; emotional and cognitive development; the role of religion-based cultural symbols, meanings, and practices; and psychological experiences. There are cases where individuals have reached maturity in physical and psychological development but are at a state of infancy in faith development. It is also true that individuals can reach a higher state of faith development prior to reaching full physical and psychological maturity.

Primal faith occurs from birth until the age of two. During the first two years of a child's development physical and neurological growth is happening at a faster rate than any other stage. Most child psychologists would articulate that by twelve weeks of age a child is capable of visual and auditory responses to various levels of stimuli. At sixteen weeks these same children are able to hold up their heads as an alert to something catching their attention. By nine months children can intentionally move toward stimuli, and by one year they can interact with stimuli for three to five minutes and obtain object permanence. These first two years are also when attachment begins. As stated earlier, children require three points of contact in their community in order to succeed. The first relationship children foster are their parents, and every relationship

5. Fowler, *Stages of Faith*.

Developmental Considerations

after will find its foundation in how the parent-child relationship is developed in these first few years. This includes relationships to the child's faith development.[6]

The Intuitive-Projective Faith stage occurs at the start of age two with the development of symbolic thought processes and representational play. This means that children at this stage in faith development are focused on the teachings, stories, and images presented to them by those they are most influenced by—their parents. This stage is marked by the child's ability to run with their imagination. In faith development, this stage conjures the foundation of the child's perception of moral values based on beliefs of the overarching authority in their lives.[7]

During the first two stages in a child's moral, cognitive, and faith development is when emotional intelligence finds its cornerstone. In the first eight years of a child's life is when habitual emotional reaction develops in a child, resulting in their personal response to high-stress situations. In these years children learn the basics of their moral faith and the basic rules of society through school, religious engagement, and community involvement. Based on Kohlberg's theory, interests at this stage will begin with not understanding the difference between punishments and doing the right thing and shift to desiring rewards rather than punishment. They learn to sit still, to speak when spoken to, to act in the specific ways that are inherent to their social norms. These two stages also form the foundational basis for their relationships in the future. A child whose relationships at home are based on trust and forgiveness will develop healthier relationships as an adult than a child whose relationships at home are based on neglect and mistrust. Emotional intelligence development is essential to the overall growth of a child. Stages one and two of development will form the foundation and determine whether a child will withhold emotional responses until they have an emotional outburst or will healthily express their emotions to those around them.

---

6. Roehikepartain et al., *Handbook of Spiritual Development*, 183–93.
7. Fowler, *Stages of Faith*, 56.

The Mythic-Literal Faith stage is when the beliefs and moral values taught to a child in the intuitive-projective faith stage begin to become their own observances. This stage is typically associated with age eight but can vary depending on the cognitive individuality of the child. This stage begins to remove the imagination aspect of faith and turns to the literal interpretation and one-dimensional meanings of passages and teachings. Children tend to rely on fairness and reciprocity as the tools needed to construct their own personal environment. The reality of this mindset results in possible controlling behaviors or the overtly righteous demeanor of the child. This stage has a flowing ending, as the ability to become disillusioned by the teachings that have largely ruled behavior and to apply critical thinking to the lessons and social norms that guided them up to this point happen at different stages of age development.[8]

This stage, in many ways, creates a permanent contribution to providing meaning in a child's life. In this stage of life, children and adolescents tend not to look deeper than the middle of the road in their life journey. They rarely look ahead or make connections to their reactions from past experiences. Critical thought to their existence is largely beyond their scope of comprehension. The saying goes that perception is law, and in the eyes of a child in this stage of development, there are few truer words. Interestingly, children will migrate through two of Kohlberg's stages during these years of early childhood. In the earlier years of this stage, a child's moral compass will be derived from their desire for approval from the authority figures around them. In the later years of this stage, a child's moral compass is driven by the desire to maintain social order and the rules that have already been set. As stated previously, because these developmental milestones occur so quickly over a four-to-five-year span, these developmental years can have a lasting effect on a child's understanding of right and wrong. Thus, this stage can affect their faith development in later years.

The final relevant stage to faith development in children is Synthetic-Conventional Faith. This stage is marked by a person's

8. Fowler, *Stages of Faith*, 101-8.

Developmental Considerations

ability to perceive their worldview beyond that of their parents or caregivers. Typically attributed to around the age of twelve years, this stage can occur sooner or later, depending on the child's personal development. This stage is where faith is often grown into a foundation for other areas of life, such as school, work, community programs, etc. In Kohlberg's theory this stage is where children begin to developmental separate the definition of morally right and the definition of legally right.[9] It can also be the stage where faith is lost and relationships with a higher power such as God are dismissed. This stage incorporates the ability of a child to analyze their past experiences and their anticipated future to form a faith-based environment that suits their needs. The detriment to this stage occurs when the preachings of the past become hindered, halted, or tainted by those the child deems in control or in charge.[10] Meaning, if the person in control or in charge is abusive in nature the child will become disillusioned with a faith-based foundation in growth and may let go of religion all together. In situations where transgressions of the past have not been healed and worked through, the events become foundations that inhibit the growth and use of cognitive abilities in the tasks of self-identity during this stage. These situations lead to schisms in the identity and the ideology of the individual that directly attribute to relationships to self and others in adulthood.

While the fourth stage of faith development theory is not necessarily relevant to the child's experience and is more involved in the adult's perspective, the transition to stage four is relevant to a child's development. Transition from stage three to stage four occurs when individuality is tensioned by the desire to be part of a larger group. Subjectivity is put against objectivity in the process of critical reflection. Self-fulfillment and self-actualization become priorities over the needs of others. Finally, the determination of whether they are committed to relative thought or absolute thought becomes more pronounced in their decision-making.[11]

9. Fowler, *Stages of Faith*, 232.
10. Fowler, *Stages of Faith*, 69.
11. Fowler, *Stages of Faith*, 78.

Trust Their Struggle

This transition is where adolescents and adults have begun to determine their identity in faith.

Faith development is grounded in the idea that our faith is linked to our worldviews' perspectives of right and wrong or moral development. Every stage of this theory has the potential to influence a child's life choices positively or negatively. How a child moves through each of these phases directly impacts how they interact with anxiety, depression, and suicidal ideation. In stage one, the child is developing their first interpersonal relationships with the guiding adults around them. During this stage, crucial relationship-building is essential to positive relationships in the future. The trauma of parental loss or parental indifference put the child at a higher risk of mental health disorders in the future. In the same way, indifference to the growth of their faith and thereby their basis for their understanding of right and wrong, or good and evil, in stage two can have a lasting effect on how their worldview impacts their relationship with God in stage three. Every stage is interconnected and determined by the relationships of those who are guiding them through each stage.

Childhood spirituality as a developmental philosophy is a neuropsychological understanding that links experiences, perspectives, and concepts from infancy through adulthood to spiritual growth.[12] Religious and spiritual experiences are impacted by developmental changes in a similar way that thoughts and behaviors are impacted by developmental changes. There are not many studies that corroborate spiritual development and its link to brain development. Most sources are linked to Fowler's understanding of child development. Overall, there are three main areas of focus in child development linked to spiritual development. These are undifferentiated spirituality, developmental spirituality, and operational spirituality.[13]

---

12. King et al., *Handbook of Spiritual Development*, 189.

13. Currently there are several ways in which different individuals and organizations utilize and define the term spirituality. In this context, spirituality is defined as an individual's relationship to their soul.

Developmental Considerations

The undifferentiated spirituality stage is linked to Fowler's Primal Faith developmental stage. This stage in spirituality occurs in the first four years of development. A primary requirement for spirituality is interconnectedness. A child's ability to build interconnected relationships is greatly impacted by this stage in development and their relationship with their caregivers. Deprivation of development toward trust, hope, and love in this stage can result in a lack of an ability to interconnect on a spiritual level. At this stage, many scholars dictate that there can be no spiritual development due to a lack of cognitive development at this age. However, the foundation for a relationship with self is developed at this stage through how they form a relationship with their caregivers and therefore holds an important role in the development of spirituality.[14] If there is a lack of development at this stage in the development process, the individual can begin to isolate themselves from their environment. Likewise, if there is a traumatic event during this stage, an infant's sense of safety in their environment becomes compromised.

The effects of trauma on a child's development differ depending on their environment. Two infants can experience the same event, but only one may respond with trauma-based behaviors. If the child has the existence of a constant, caring, protective, and trusted caregiver then the child may not experience any long-term or even short-term effects of the trauma.[15]

The next stage is the developmental spirituality stage, which occurs over the course of several years, leading from around the age of five years until they intellectually reach the operational spirituality stage. This stage is reached when the infant moves into their academic phase in life's stages. This stage is categorized by interpersonal relationships expanding beyond the family unit. This stage occurs within two phases that are subcategorized under a single stage due to their flexibility in age requirement during development. It is critical to the overall development of a child's spirituality that they engage with each phase positively. During

---

14. King et al., *Handbook of Spiritual Development*, 190.
15. "How Early Childhood Trauma Is Unique," 1.

this stage children begin to internalize lessons that are taught to them by the people they built relationships with in the first phase. The tangible thought phase is the first phase in this stage. This phase emphasizes the reality of the five senses and their necessity for thoughts to become factual. For example, a child molding a piece of clay from a ball into a snake would understand that the mass and weight of the clay has not altered—simply the shape has. At this phase in spiritual development children often look to the relationships they formed during the undifferentiated spiritual stage and the examples their caregivers are setting. A child who enters this stage with a caregiver who practices personal spiritual development may be more likely to develop spiritual growth faster than a child whose caregivers do not. Spirituality at this phase is more experiential and based on exposures to stories, interpersonal influences, and an intuitive understanding of right and wrong. The more involved of exposure to spiritual development and self-worth a child is exposed to during this phase will directly influence how developed their spiritual experimentation will be in the next phase of the developmental spirituality stage.

The formal operations and abstract ideas phase is the second phase in the development spirituality stage.[16] This is the first step in a child's development where the child begins to branch out into their own identity in their spiritual development. In many cases, this phase of spiritual development is linked to their religious development but not always. In this phase the child begins to develop a sense of self and begins exploring what the self means to them. The caregiver's influence remains the cornerstone of their development, but in this phase, peers begin to influence spiritual behaviors as well. It is in this phase where many children begin to experiment with different spiritual practices such as meditation, prayer, deep contemplation of self-worth, and communication with a higher being. This phase is also marked by the literal interpretation of teachings which can lead to misunderstandings and mistrust of spirituality practices. This stage is also marked by impatience for outcomes in spiritual practices. For example, a child who is learning to meditate

---

16. Piaget et al., *Psychology of the Child*, 139–43.

Developmental Considerations

in order to control their anxiety might become frustrated when the desired results are not immediately presented.

Trauma experienced during this phase with the absence of a stable and loving caregiver environment can have a detrimental impact on the spiritual development of the adolescent. In addition to the many physical and psychological developmental delays that may occur, spiritual development may deteriorate in the form of lack of self-confidence, self-understanding, and self-care. Children who experience trauma during this phase may develop child traumatic stress: "Children who suffer from child traumatic stress are those who have been exposed to one or more traumas over the course of their lives and develop reactions that persist and affect their daily lives after the events have ended."[17] In many cases the children who experience these traumas at this age experience them within the family unit and are unidentified by caregivers or outside individuals. These traumas are also sometimes not maintained in conscious memory by the child as they develop; however, they continue to have responses due to a subconscious reaction. Early intervention with spiritual self-care practices have demonstrated positive effects in combatting these behaviors.[18]

The developmental spirituality stage encompasses the majority of the adolescent years and can be where an adolescent remains through adulthood. Ultimately, many individuals never make it past this stage in development toward spiritual understanding and wellness. However, in the event that a child is guided through spiritual practices and spiritual health, they would move into the operational spirituality stage in spiritual development.

The operational spirituality stage is categorized by the dedicated practice of spiritual maturity in a youth and the reflection of meaning and conflicts between their personal understanding of self as it pertains to their faith and what they have been taught up until this point. In this stage, youth are now practicing spiritual growth as part of a routine and have matured past the stage of questioning the practice. In this stage the adolescent will see the

---

17. "How Early Childhood Trauma Is Unique," 1.
18. See chapter four case study.

divine being as abstract and will have a deeper sense of self. This stage emphasizes personal positive growth and understanding. While this stage is categorized by new ideas, these ideas are built on the questioning and restructuring of ideas that were founded in the previous stages of spiritual development. This is the most complex stage of spiritual development in an individual's lifetime because of the extensive additional factors in this overall developmental stage. The operational spirituality stage takes place at the same instance as biological maturation and sexual exploration. In this developmental time, peer-to-peer influences become primary in many cases to caregiver influence. Caregiver influence will always remain the foundation on which their understanding of their own existence has been developed but at this stage; the peer relationship begins to manipulate and change the ideas of those foundations, forming the new sense of self. The conformist alteration and the deeper understanding of expectations and judgements can hinder the development of independent spiritual growth during this stage.[19]

The operational spirituality stage ends when the individual has matured to an unalterable perspective of their own spiritual practice and understanding.[20] While changes may occur in the adult stages of spirituality, by the end of adolescence, typically the age of neurological maturity, the beliefs and practices of their spiritual growth have become embedded in permanency. Exceptions can be made for traumatic life events such as a car accident or near-death experience where the brain begins to re-examine the known and unknown of their own existence.

Spiritual development is a personal journey that can be experienced outside the parameters of childhood and adolescent growth. However, the more mature the individual becomes neurologically, the more difficult the acceptance of new ideas and practices becomes. Proverbs 22:6: "Train up a child in the way he should go: and when he is old, he will not depart from it."

---

19. King et al., *Handbook of Spiritual Development*, 191.
20. King et al., *Handbook of Spiritual Development*, 192.

Developmental Considerations

Undifferentiated spirituality, developmental spirituality, and operational spirituality stages are each crucial to the development of a child. Trauma during any stage of spiritual development in early childhood and leading into adolescents can have a lasting negative effect on an individual's ability to connect on a spiritual level to self-care and a higher being and purpose. Early intervention of spiritual self-care practices led by pastoral counselors in the early years of neurological development may have a positive impact on an individual's ability to cope with stress, anxiety, depression, and suicidal ideation brought on by traumatic events or genetic influences.

3 ———————————————————

Cultural Considerations and World Application

"Because all of you are one in the Messiah Jesus, a person is no longer a Jew or a Greek, a slave or a free person, a male or a female. And if you belong to the Messiah, then you are Abraham's descendants indeed, and heirs according to the promise."

—Gal 3:28–29

ALTHOUGH SUICIDE IS A serious public health problem spanning every developed country, there are very few, if any, real initiatives to combat suicide proactively by leading government agencies or even religious organizations. More than 700,000 individuals succeed in suicide worldwide every year. This number does not include those who attempt but fail. Suicide is the third leading cause of death worldwide among youth ages fifteen to nineteen and the second leading cause of death among developed countries overall.

Intervention is essential to prevent suicides among our youth populations. Evidence-based studies have come out of several developed countries, indicating positive results when stress

Cultural Considerations and World Application

management and anxiety management exercises are introduced to adolescents. However, the only countries with any indication of attempting a public transformation to a more mental health-friendly approach to adolescent care are Ireland and Australia. Unfortunately, the results of these programs that were implemented are inconclusive, with Ireland seeing a decline in suicides among youth but Australia maintaining an upwards incline. More studies will need to be conducted in order to determine if it is the program or the delivery of the program that is the issue.

With the government largely taking a backseat to suicide prevention, it has become the mission of many private organizations to take up the mantle and attempt a shift in societal norms. The Christian church should be proactively leading the nation in suicide prevention care through spiritual self-care programs that teach and promote anxiety and stress management exercises while actively finding our connection to the divine. This chapter will review some of the initiatives currently being implemented in near-peer countries to the United States. This chapter serves to show where many of the implemented initiatives for the Kindness Project find their standard.

Japan

The culture in Japan is heavily diverse in its beliefs, practices, and cultural norms. Many of the countries' practices and beliefs trace back to the earliest writings in history. Suicide in Japan is no exception. Japan has several beliefs that structure suicide as a virtuous act to atone for sinful behavior. The culture focuses on the group as a whole taking precedence over individual needs or desires. Japan prioritizes maintaining harmony within a group culture, even at the expense of individual freedoms. In addition, the Japanese are also very conscience of how they are perceived by their peers. Shame and social distancing are the primary reactions of peers to unfavorable actions. These reactions can extend passed the individual to family and associates as well. Understanding the view that an individual is responsible for restoring the social

Trust Their Struggle

standing of the group—and that the group is more important than the individual—brings to light the cultural acceptance of suicide in Japan. Historically, the most severe act that individuals take to restore the social standing of the group is suicide.[1]

Suicide of resolve or *kakugo no jisatsu* is traced back to the samurai. The samurai are an ancient warrior class in Japan. Suicide was often used by the samurai as a show of loyalty and was considered an honorable course of action to clear an individual of guilt. Many times, these acts of suicide would be done in a ceremonial form such as Seppuku, which translates to "cut stomach." Seppuku was a ritualized and glorified form of suicide in which the individual would disembowel themselves with their sword in order to atone for sins and maintain social status for themselves and their community.[2] The most enlightening legend in Japan that glorifies suicide as an act of redemption is the story of Ronin. In this legend, the government orders the feudal lord to commit suicide after the feudal lord draws his sword against an official of the court. This incites a plot by the forty-seven retainers of the feudal lord to avenge their master. The story ends with the forty-seven retainers killing the official and then committing seppuku for breaking the law.[3]

Shinju is another form of historical culturally acceptable suicide and translates to "depths of the heart." The practice was utilized as a way of avoiding being undutiful to their parents and thereby bringing shame on the group as a whole, while still demonstrating their love and commitment to one another.

It is important to note that officially ritualistic suicides are no longer practiced. However, there are still examples of individuals and couples participating in this practice in modern society. In some cases, psychologists have utilized the historical context of suicide in Japan to understand why some individuals commit suicide today.

1. Russell et al., "Cultural Influences on Suicide in Japan," 2–5.
2. Fuse, "Suicide and Culture in Japan," 57–63.
3. Russell et al., "Cultural Influences on Suicide in Japan," 2–5.

Current Statistics on Youth Suicide

Suicide is the number one cause of death among youth in Japan. Up until the year 2020, there was a large knowledge gap regarding the demographics and factors associated with suicide among youth in Japan. A study conducted by Shinichiro Nagamitsu, et al., sought to explore this gap through a population-based questionnaire survey. The survey was administered to 22,419 youth between the ages of thirteen and eighteen years of age. The questionnaire consisted of twenty-nine items that covered the emotional status, family function, cyberbullying, suicidality, and stressors linked to relationships, performance, and sexual identity.[4] Of those that completed the survey,

> The prevalence of suicidal ideation was 21.6% in males and 28.5% in females, and that of attempted suicide was 3.5% in males and 6.6% and in females. Bullying and stress related to family relationships had the strongest associations with suicidality. Exposure to cyberbullying had the highest odds ratio for both junior high (3.1, 95% confidence interval [CI] 2.1–4.4) and high school students (3.6, 95% CI 2.5–5.3). Other factors significantly associated with suicidality were sex, emotional status, and stress about relationships with friends, sexual identity, school records, and academic course. Adolescents accessed a variety of resources to cope with stressors, with the Internet being the most common resource consulted.[5]

Another study conducted in 2016 by Sun Y. Jeon, et al., explored suicide in both Japan and South Korea. This study found that suicide in Japan has increased by 20 percent between 1985 and 2010. The study collected data through national statistic organizations. The study focused their search on five-year increments and "fitted the series of intrinsic estimator age-period-cohort models to estimate the effects of age-related processes, secular

---

4. Nagamitsu et al., *Prevalence and Associated Factors of Suicidality*, 2.
5. Nagamitsu et al., *Prevalence and Associated Factors of Suicidality*, 1.

changes, and birth cohort dynamics."[6] The study concluded that the elevated rates in Japan were elevated after the Asian financial crisis in the late 1990s. The relevance of this study is the demonstrated elevating trend in suicide throughout Japan between 1985 and 2010.[7]

A final study worth noting for the purposes of exploring current suicide trends in Japan is a study done by E. Yoshioka, et. al. This study explored time trends in method specific suicide in Japan between 1990 and 2011. This study was conducted in 2014 and was published by the University of Cambridge. The researchers utilized statistics gathered by the Vital Statistics of Japan as a basis for their research. The study divided the methods utilized to commit suicide into seven categories: overdose, gases, hanging, drowning, cutting, jumping, and miscellaneous. They then further divided the categories into age groups: 15–24, 25–44, 45–64 and 65+ years. The results of this study demonstrated a rise in suicide for all age groups through the late 1990s. This may be contributed to the financial crisis in Japan in the 1990s. After the year 2000, the study observed a more dramatic increase in the 15–24 and 25–44 age groups than in the older age groups across both male and female gender groups.[8]

The studies conducted on suicide trends in Japan are minimal. Most of the studies conducted are based on the same data groupings from the Vital Statistics of Japan and explore this data set from different perspectives. None of the studies conducted prior to the study done in 2020 by Shinichiro Nagamitsu, et al., explored suicide in Japan from a human perspective, nor did they collaborate the information from the statistics with the current programs available to combat rising suicide rates among youth or any other age group. However, the necessary notation that there is a significant and concerning rise in suicide among youth is made in each study, both provided here and not.

---

6. Jeon et al., "Population-Based Analysis," 356.
7. Jeon et al., "Population-Based Analysis," 356.
8. Yoshioka et al., "Time Trends in Method-Specific Suicide Rates," 58–68.

Cultural Considerations and World Application

Current Programs

The Japanese government and other institutions within Japan have taken necessary steps to address the public health crisis of suicide. In October of 2006 Japan's Basic Act for Suicide Prevention was successfully implemented into action, and it was again revised in 2016. The act solidified combating rising suicide rates as an overarching government policy whose responsibility is not limited to any one specific organization or ministry.[9] In addition, a new series of policies were established in Japan in 2009 that were created to prevent suicide. These policies included an expansion of unemployment insurance, improving safety nets for economically disadvantaged families, and tighter regulations on temporal employment.[10]

Among the non-governmental organizations in Japan, the most robust program worth noting is the Nippon Foundation Suicide Prevention Project. This project is broken down into three separate stages or components. The first is to formulate implementation models with the local governments to prevent suicide. In this stage, the Nippon Foundation collaborated with the local small government organizations as well as the Japan government to revise the Basic Act on Suicide Countermeasures. The revision occurred in 2016, and the organization input the stipulation that all prefectures, cities, towns, and villages would now be required to implement suicide countermeasure strategies. The organization went into negotiations with the understanding that each location would require a unique approach based on their cultural and societal norms.[11]

The second stage was to implement countermeasures against suicide by adolescents. In this stage, the Nippon Foundation established two separate avenues of approach to combating suicide in a proactive manner. The first is a program titled Light Ring; a non-profit organization that focuses on friends, partners, and family members of individuals experiencing suicidal ideation and

---

9. "Suicide Prevention" (WHO).
10. "Suicide Prevention in Japan."
11. Nippon Foundation Suicide Prevention Project

depression. The program's goal is to encourage family and friends into a space of understanding while illuminating helpful and non-helpful behaviors of caregivers. The program's aim is to focus on helping the individual suffering from suicidal ideation and depression through encouraging family members to take a reassuring but not facilitating role in the lives of the sufferer. Through this practice, the individual would not become reliant on the caregiver but, instead, would care for themselves under the support of the caregivers. This organization also serves as a link to resources for therapy and counseling services and aims to reduce the cultural norm that requesting help is an indication of weakness. The second avenue of approach is the establishment of an Internet-based crisis intervention model called OVA. This organization focuses on the use of technology-based programs such as search-linked advertising to provide consultation and support to those who search for specific terminology such as "I want to die." The program would then automatically reach out to the individual via chat functions or telephone calls once they have been identified through the search analytics function with information assistance and services.[12]

The third stage of the program is surveying and public awareness related to suicide. The survey was conducted in 2016 and included forty thousand individuals nationwide. The survey focused on the individuals' experience with suicide, suicidal ideation, and depression. In some cases, the subject answered as the one experiencing mental illness, and in some cases, the subject answered as a caregiver.[13]

The implementation of the Basic Act on Suicide Countermeasures increased the implementation of local level suicide prevention programs. However, a study conducted by Naohiro Yonemoto, et al., demonstrated a need for learning objectives for the organizations and the local populace as to why these programs are important as well as higher-level evaluation of these programs to ensure effectiveness. The study created a database of every localized program offered across Japan and explored how they

12. Nippon Foundation, *1 in 4 People Contemplate Suicide*, 1
13. Nippon Foundation, *1 in 4 People Contemplate Suicide*, 1

implement their programs, how effectively the program advertises, and how the organization measures their effectivity toward a decline in suicide.[14]

Japan has taken extensive measures in the last five years to produce a program that would address the rising number of suicides among adolescents and young adults in their country. The programs implemented are new and will take time to establish their effectiveness in getting the yearly number of suicides to decline.

One of the most common forms of spiritual self-care in Japan is forest bathing. This practice was invented in the 1980s by Professor Yoshifumi when he conducted a study on why we feel relaxed when we encounter nature. The term was coined by the Japanese government and is based on ancient Shinto and Buddhist practices. The Japanese government has set aside forty-eight office "forest therapy" trails that are designated areas for forest bathing. They have also funded more than $4 million in research associated with mental health regulation and forest bathing practices.[15]

European Union

Suicide culture in most European countries is met with shame, fear, guilt, and uneasiness. In many European countries the twentieth century was the first to see religious sanctions removed from acts of suicide. This meant that suicidal actions were no longer criminalized. Suicide is often perceived as a taboo subject that should not be discussed in public settings. However, with the advent of the twentieth century, studies and programs began development in many of these countries, as individuals began noticing an upward trend in anxiety, depression, and suicidal ideation across all age groups.

---

14. Yonemoto et al., "Implementation of Gatekeeper Training Programs," 2.
15. "Origin of Forest Bathing and Forest Therapy," 1.

Current Statistics on Youth Suicide

Suicide in European countries has been on the rise across each country. The average ratio of suicide rates in the European Union is 13.74 suicides per 100,000 with the highest rates in the Mediterranean area. The country with the highest suicide ratings was Lithuania, which reached an average of 30 suicides per 100,000.[16] Understanding the statistics of just a few of these European countries can give a better understanding of the overall picture of suicide in the European Union.

Suicide in Germany, like so many other countries, has been on the rise since 2007. Similar to other countries, the discussion of suicide has not been studied to exhaustion. One study found looked at the underlying reasons and spatiotemporal risk patterns of suicide between 2007 and 2011.[17] This study looked at a total of 48,570 suicides that occurred between 2007 and 2011 across Germany. The results demonstrated an overall increase from 11.4 deaths per 100,000 persons to 12.6 deaths per 100,000 persons. Interestingly, this study did note that there seemed to be no correlation between suicide ratings and the availability of professional therapists when broken down into regional statistics.[18,19] A study concentrated on suicide in Lithuania found that in 2014 there was a trend among youth aged nine to nineteen years that resulted in a rise from 4.8 per 100,000 persons to 13.7 per 100,000 persons.[20] The concerning factor for Lithuania is the school-based suicide education program established by the country and the continued rise in suicide in the country. In a study conducted by UNICEF, Ireland was ranked fourth out of the European Union countries in youth suicide statistics, with 10.3 per 100,000 persons among youth aged fifteen to nineteen years.[21]

16. Gutiérrez-Barroso et al., "Suicide in Europe Countries," 1–10.
17. Helbich et al., "Spatiotemporal Suicide Risk in Germany," 1–8.
18. Helbich et al., "Spatiotemporal Suicide Risk in Germany," 1–8.
19. Kapusta et al., "Rural-Urban Differences in Austrian Suicides," 311–18.
20. Stricka and Jakubauskiene, "Suicide Prevention," 1.
21. "Ireland's Teen Suicide Rate," 1.

Cultural Considerations and World Application

An overall study conducted by the Organization for Economic Co-operation and Development (OECD) found that the countries with the highest suicide rates among teens in 2015 were Canada, Estonia, Latvia, Iceland, and New Zealand. These countries each had a suicide statistic of 10/100,000 or higher. Contrasting this outcome, the countries of Greece, Israel, Italy, Portugal, and Spain all had youth suicide rates of 3/100,000 or less.[22]

Current Programs

In most European countries, strategies for suicide prevention can be separated into two separate approaches: health care and public health.[23] One of the European Union's primary courses of action to combat suicide among their population is education resources on suicide prevention. Interestingly, not every country in the European Union has a national suicide prevention program.[24] In a collaborative effort to combat suicide among youth in European countries, ten countries participated in a program titled Saving and Empowering Young Lives in Europe (SEYLE) project. The eleven countries that participated were Austria, Estonia, France, Germany, Hungary, Ireland, Italy, Romania, Slovenia, Spain, and Sweden. The project was created to promote mental health and healthy lifestyles, while preventing psychopathology and suicidal behaviors among adolescents.[25]

During this program, several preventative programs were put into place in a controlled setting for students. The study sample of 11,110 students from across 168 schools in 11 countries looked at three different preventative programs against one control group to determine effectiveness.

The first program was Question, Persuade, Refer (QPR). This is a United States-developed program that focuses on training

---

22. "CO4.4: Teenage Suicides."
23. "World Health Report: 2002."
24. "World Health Report: 2002."
25. Wasserman, "Review of Health and Risk-Behaviours," 1093.

gatekeepers to identify and intervene when adolescents demonstrate the risk behaviors associated with anxiety, depression, or suicidal ideation. For the purposes of the SEYLE study, the trained individuals were teachers and other school staff.[26]

The second program implemented was the Youth Aware of Mental Health (YAM) program. The YAM program is based on an educational approach to mental health. The program covers six topics that the adolescent would be educated on. These topics are awareness of mental health and health/risk behaviors, self-help advice, stress and crisis, depression, and suicidal thoughts, helping a troubled friend, and getting advice—who to contact. These lessons are then combined with role play sessions.

The third program in the study was professional screening. This program is used to help health professionals identify adolescents that are at-risk for suicidal behaviors. This is done through a questionnaire that is given to the students. Students who score at or above a cut offline are referred for clinical assessment.[27]

The final group in the study was a control group. This group of students would be exposed only to posters hanging in the classroom environment. This group was also provided contact information and resources for acquiring assistance if needed.[28]

The study randomly assigned the 168 schools a preventative intervention measure. Forty schools were assigned the QPR program, 45 schools were assigned the YAM program, 43 schools were assigned the professional screening program, and 40 schools were assigned as the control groups. The program utilized four different rating scales to determine reliability of the results. These included the Beck Depression Inventory, Zung Self-Rating Anxiety Scale, Strengths and Difficulties Questionnaire, and WHO-Five Well-Being Index. The conclusion of the study found that the Youth Aware of Mental Health model produced the highest reduction of incident suicide attempts.[29] The article did not indicate whether

26. Wasserman, "Review of Health and Risk-Behaviours," 1100.
27. Wasserman, "Review of Health and Risk-Behaviours," 1101.
28. Wasserman, "Review of Health and Risk-Behaviours," 1101.
29. Wasserman, "Review of Health and Risk-Behaviours," 1104.

Cultural Considerations and World Application

any of the schools that participated in this program continued to implement the programs in the district following the conclusion of the study.

The European countries that are currently known to host national suicide prevention programs are Belarus, Bulgaria, Czech Republic, Denmark, Estonia, Finland, France, Hungary, Ireland, Latvia, Lithuania, Norway, Romania, Slovenia, Sweden, Turkey, and the United Kingdom.[30] The majority of the intervention programs that are utilized in these countries are school-based programs. Based on analysis of the 2002 World Health Organization study between countries with national programs and countries without national programs, there does not seem to be a significant effect on suicide rates in these countries. For example, Lithuania has one of the most extensive national suicide prevention programs in the European Union but also holds the highest suicide rates.

Canada

There is a unique perspective for suicide that comes from Canada's culture because of the extensive diversity spread across the country. Canada is made up of native peoples and immigrants from all over the world living together. Extensive studies have been conducted on the topic of suicide. Reports can be found on suicide methodology, suicide analysis of various demographics, and overall suicide statistics leading into the year 2020. However, there are no peer-reviewed statistical studies demonstrating data on preventative programs in Canada.

Statistics

In Canada, like other nations, suicide is the second leading cause of death among adolescents aged ten to twenty-four. Suicide accounts for about 2 percent of annual deaths in Canada since the

---

30. World Health Organization, *World Health Report 2002*.

1970s.[31] Between 1960 and 1991 there was a 4.5 percent increase in males and a 3 percent increase in females aged fifteen to nineteen.[32] This upward trend in suicides would eventually see a decline. One study found that the suicide rate among Canadians fifteen years and older had decreased from 14.4/100,000 to 12.6/100,000 between 2000 and 2011.[33] Another study published in the *Canadian Medical Association Journal* found that the nation-side suicide statistic for 2018 fell to around 11.7/100,000.[34] Overall Canada has seen a substantial decline in suicides leading into 2018.

According to a study conducted by the government of Canada, males are three times more likely to attempt suicide than females, approximately 11 people day every day from suicide, and approximately 4,000 people day each year. Between 2017 and 2018, approximately 250/100,000 youth were hospitalized due to self-inflicted injury.[35] Despite the number of successful suicides being on the decline, there is some concern surrounding the abnormally high number of attempted suicide and self-inflicted injury resulting in hospitalization.

Current Programs

Canada belongs to the G8 country forum which consists of eight highly industrialized countries. This is an organization initially formed by Russia in 1997. The current countries of this forum include France, Germany, Italy, the United Kingdom, Japan, the United States, Canada, and Russia. Currently, Canada is the only member of this program that does not have a national suicide prevention strategy of any kind. The Canadian Association for Suicide

---

31. Canadian Mental Health Association, *Reconciliation and Mental.*
32. "Canadian Mental Health Association on Reconciliation."
33. Skinner et al., "Suicide in Canada."
34. Liu et al., "Changes over Time in Means of Suicide."
35. "Suicide in Canada: Key Statistics."

Prevention (CASP) has been calling for a national strategy since the 1990s.[36]

Canada's most involved suicide prevention organization is CASP. This organization provides classes and events to help bring awareness to suicide among all age groups in Canada. Currently there are no programs that are hosted by local schools on a mandatory regular basis for youth to participate in. Any program that does take place has to be at the initiative of the students or their caregivers. CASP's current primary focus in on building a national suicide prevention program.

Another organization in Canada that focuses on suicide prevention is the Mental Health Commission of Canada. They are an information-based organization whose website provides a myriad of resources for those seeking assistance with suicidal ideation. One of the programs that this organization promotes is called Roots of Hope. This program is built on a five-pillar system that helps communities implement their own suicide prevention program.

The first pillar is Specialized Support. This pillar focuses on peer support, group support, interventions, and access to services. This pillar is largely about finding a program that works for the individual. The second pillar is Training and Networks. This pillar focuses on training the gatekeepers. The third pillar is Public Awareness Campaigns, which focus on raising awareness about the program that was developed. Means-Safety is the fourth pillar. This one focuses on implementing the program in areas of the community where suicide is highest. The final pillar is Research. This pillar focuses on a way to study the success or failure of the program that was implemented. There are a few private organizations that provide suicide prevention certifications in Canada; however there is not a nationally recognized program. The private programs offered include ASIST, SafeTALK, and Mental Health first aid.

---

36. Olson, "Suicide and Stigma."

Australia

Suicide has been a long-standing problem in Australia, as it is in many parts of the world. The number of deaths by suicide in Australia has continuously increased over the twenty-first century. In recent years the government in Australia has worked tirelessly to develop a program that will help in lowering their number one cause of death. Part of this initiative was the establishment of the National Suicide and Self-Harm Monitoring System. This program allows for three main objectives: to explain the nature and extent of suicidal and self-harm behaviors, to improve the quality and breadth of data available to help identify trends, emerging areas of concern, and to inform responses; and to highlight those who are at increased risk of suicidal ideation.[37]

Statistics

Suicide is the number one leading cause of death for adolescents between ages five and seventeen in Australia.[38] The Australian Bureau of Statistics reported 305 suicides of children ages five to seventeen between 2010 and 2014. Aboriginal and Torres Strait Islander children comprised 84 of these deaths.[39] This same report pulled data from the Kids' Helpline on calls related to suicide. The report found that over the period from 2012 to 2016, 59,053 relevant counseling contacts were made. Of these contacts, 82.9% reported suicidal thoughts or fears, 3.2% reported immediate intent, 1.5% reported a current attempt at the time of making contact, and 12.4% were calling on behalf of someone they were worried about.[40] Interestingly, 85% of those calls were females, but males make up the higher percentage of successful suicides in Australia. In 2019, there were 12.9 per 100,000 deaths reported. When

---

37. "3.3 National Suicide Prevention Strategy," 1.
38. Kinchin and Doran, "Cost of Youth Suicide in Australia," 672.
39. "Understanding Suicide, Suicide Attempts and Self-Harm," 1.
40. "Understanding Suicide, Suicide Attempts and Self-Harm," 1.

Cultural Considerations and World Application

broken down by gender, 19.8 per 100,000 suicides were by males, and 6.3 suicides were by females.[41]

Current Programs

Australia was one of the first nations in the world to adopt a national youth suicide prevention strategy in 1995. This strategy would be replaced with the National Suicide Prevention Strategy or NSPS in 2000. The NSPS had two main goals in its establishment. The first was to adopt a community-based approach that would enhance public understanding of suicide. The second is to increase the support and care available to citizens and communities affected by suicide or suicidal behavior.[42] There are six main objectives laid out on the report: "build individual resilience and the capacity for self-help, improve community strength, resilience and capacity in suicide prevention, provide targeted suicide prevention activities, implement standards and quality in suicide prevention, take a coordinated approach to suicide prevention, and to improve the evidence base and understanding of suicide prevention."[43]

One of Australia's initiatives is referred to as Headspace Schools. This program is a caregiver-based program that has a four-step approach to suicide prevention. The four steps are Prevention, Early Intervention, Intervention, and Postvention. Headspace offers programs in mental health, physical health, alcohol and other drug services, and work and study support. Their program is both easily accessible through a virtual platform as well as available in most schools across Australia. The program is only available to persons aged 12 to 25.[44]

Another of the initiatives implemented in Australia is called EveryMind. This program operates under a theory that everyone should help in suicide prevention. This program has been

41. "Suicide & Self-Harm Monitoring," 1.
42. "3.3 National Suicide Prevention Strategy," 1.
43. "3.3 National Suicide Prevention Strategy," 1.
44. "Understanding Suicide, Suicide Attempts and Self-Harm," 1.

approved by the World Health Organization. This program has several approaches. The first is called Mind Frame. Mind Frame is an initiative to combat inaccurate information on Mental Illness in Australian Mass Media. The second initiative is Life in Mind. The purpose of this initiative is to connect all of the Australian-based suicide prevention programs and organizations to one another so that they can collaborate on a solution. The remaining initiatives are programs that target specific demographics such as the LGBTQ+ community, the refugee community, and support groups for individuals who attempted but did not succeed in suicide. The aim of implementing this project by the Australian government is to combat suicide through a collaborative environment; instead of each of these programs acting alone, Australia hopes that each program can work together to form a full-body approach to suicide prevention.[45]

Ireland

Ireland maintains meticulous statistical data regarding suicide in their country. The most recent study was released in January of 2021 by the National Office for Suicide Prevention. This dedication to analyzing the problem within their country has led to various studies on prevention methodology within Ireland.

Statistics

According to the National Office for Suicide Prevention in Ireland, 9.7 per 100,000 youth succeeded in suicide in 2019. Unlike other countries in the same economic world bracket, Ireland's suicide statistic for youth has consistently fallen since 2001 from its original 16.6 per 100,000. Another report released by the National Office for Suicide Prevention claimed that Ireland ranks sixteenth highest for youth suicide across European countries.[46]

---

45. EveryMind, "Your Mental Wellness."
46. "Mental Health" (Government of Ireland).

Cultural Considerations and World Application

According to 3Ts: Turn the Tide of Suicide, a private organization working to combat suicide in Ireland, despite the falling numbers in Ireland for suicide among youth, it remains the leading cause of death among male youth ages fifteen to twenty. Suicide among females in Ireland is significantly less likely. Studies have not been able to definitively determine the reason why males are more likely to succeed in suicide than females of the same age group.[47] This same organization has led the way in developing programs for suicide prevention in Ireland.

Current Programs

The government in Ireland specifically does not currently have any proactive programs. They offer informational pamphlets and organizational training on suicide prevention to educators, parents, and other societal leadership on emergency procedures for youth. There are a few organizations that offer mindfulness programs to educational institutions within the country. One study came out of Ireland that demonstrates the success of mindfulness in mental health interventions. Michelle Byre, an undergraduate student in psychology, under the supervision of Dr. John Hyland, conducted a study on mindfulness as an intervention to stress and anxiety in post-secondary schools. The study found a shift in lowering stress and anxiety among the youth who participated in the mindfulness activities.[48] The relevance of the study is in the similarities between the mindfulness activities in the study and the spiritual self-care activities in the ministry created in this study.

Similar to most developed countries in the world, suicide among youth in South Africa is a growing problem. The most recent studies to come out of South Africa on this topic are from 2018 and earlier, leaving questions about the most recent years results. Programs are lacking as governments determine the best course of action beyond statistical data for combating this problem.

---

47. "Suicide in Ireland Survey," 1.
48. Byrne, "Preliminary Outcomes of Mindfulness," 1.

Statistics

According to the Western Cape Government web page, suicide is the fastest-growing cause of death for the fifteen to twenty-four age group in South Africa. The records indicate that children as young as seven have been identified as succeeding in suicide. They've determined that 9 percent of all teen deaths in South Africa are attributed to suicide, and their statistics indicate this number rises every year.[49]

The exact statistics surrounding suicide in South Africa vary dramatically depending on the sampling procedures and the research methods utilized. They ranged anywhere from 11 to 25 per 100,000 of the population. Very few studies conducted in South Africa on suicide have addressed the problem from an age-based perspective, making separating out these statistics difficult. However, the numbers across all age groups are still alarming.[50]

Current Programs

While South Africa does not currently have a government-sanctioned solution or program for suicide prevention, several professors and professionals in the field of psychology have developed recommendations. These initiatives include "broadening the public awareness of suicide and its risk factors, enhancing population-based and clinical care services and programs, and suicide prevention through effective monitoring systems and research."[51] This study determined that this would be the only manner in which the government could truly intervene. However, the study concluded that intervention at the individual and family level to solve interpersonal conflicts was imperative. Intervention at a societal level was also included in the proposal, indicating that majority of children in South Africa have experienced some form of trauma before reaching adulthood. This, combined with a

---

49. "Anxiety, Depression, and Adolescent Suicide," 1.
50. Schlebusch, "Suicide Prevention," 435.
51. Schlebusch, "Suicide Prevention," 438.

Cultural Considerations and World Application

lack of resources available for psychiatric care, indicates a need for community-level involvement or initiatives is vital to the solution to suicide prevention in adolescents.[52]

Summary of Cultural Considerations

Although suicide is a serious public health problem spanning throughout every developed country, there are very few, if any real initiatives to combat suicide proactively by leading government agencies or even religious organizations. More than 700,000 individuals succeed in suicide worldwide every year. This number does not include those who attempt but fail. Suicide is the fourth leading cause of death worldwide among youth ages fifteen to nineteen and the second leading cause of death among developed countries overall.

Intervention is essential to prevent suicides among our youth populations. Evidence-based studies have come out of several developed countries, indicating positive results when stress management and anxiety management exercises are introduced to adolescents. However, the only countries with any indication of attempting a public transformation to a more mental health-friendly approach to adolescent care are Ireland and Australia. Unfortunately, the results of these programs that were implemented are inconclusive, with Ireland seeing a decline in suicides among youth but Australia maintaining an upwards incline. More studies will need to be conducted in order to determine if it is the program or the delivery of the program that is the issue.

With the government largely taking a back seat to suicide prevention, it has become the mission of many private organizations to take up the mantle and attempt a shift in societal norms. The Christian church should be proactively leading the nation in suicide prevention care through spiritual self-care programs that teach and promote anxiety and stress management exercises while actively finding our connection to the divine.

52. Schlebusch, "Suicide Prevention," 438.

4

Case Studies

Desire without knowledge is not good, and whoever makes haste with his feet misses his way.

—Prov 19:2

THE HUMAN SUBJECT STUDY took on two separate bodies of questioning. The first survey was given to twenty-five parents to determine observed effectivity of the project. Of the twenty-five surveys sent out, twenty-two were returned. The second survey was given to the students with parental consent to determine how the student's perceived effectiveness of the program. Of the twenty-five students requested to participate, fifteen were ultimately given parental consent to participate.

The parental survey consisted of six questions addressing the program. Each question sought to identify what type of student took the course and what the student might have derived from the program.

The survey question "What specific activity causes your child the most stress/anxiety and has your child been diagnosed with a mental health condition such as anxiety, depression, or suicidal

Case Studies

ideation?" sought to establish a baseline of what the student currently struggles with.

The survey question "Has your child developed a better understanding of anxiety/depression" sought to establish an understanding of whether the program helped the student understand mental health.

The survey question "What were the most positive results of the Kindness Project for your child, and do you believe this program will help/has helped with suicide prevention? And if so, in what way?" sought to expand on how the program might have helped with the students understanding of mental health and spiritual self-care techniques.

The survey question "Is there anything you would like to add in regard to the Kindness Project?" sought to provide the parent or guardian with an opportunity to add any additional information or thoughts on the program.

Participants whose responses were chosen for this study will be referred to by their location, the age of the child participating, and either a M to delineate a male, an F to delineate a female, or an NB to delineate non-binary.

Of those that returned the survey, nineteen stated that their students had a better understanding of anxiety and depression following the sixteen-week course. Two individuals stated no, and one stated unsure. Eight individuals had a prior mental health diagnosis while fourteen did not. There did not seem to be a correlation with a better understanding of anxiety and depression and whether or not a student had a prior mental health diagnosis.

The Kindness Project offers two separate types of classes. One is spiritually based, and one is secular-based. The primary difference between the two programs is the removal of Bible study from the class. Otherwise, all other areas of the class remain the same. Of those that returned the survey, only two participated in the secular version of the class.

Suggested improvements to the program derived from the final question in the survey included:

- Offering a class for older students. The current course is offered to five to twelve year olds.
- Only offering a faith-based program
- Offering a class that is specific to children who have a mental health diagnosis.

The most common comments regarding the most positive results of the Kindness Project for the child included:

- Helping with social anxiety.
- Understanding mental health better.
- Looking at mental health in a more positive light.
- Helping with communicating about mental health.

Of those who returned the survey, no one responded that the program does not or could not help with suicidal ideation. The most common comments regarding whether the participant believed this program would help or has helped with suicide prevention include:

- Yes because,
  - Learning about self-awareness
  - Having a toolbox for mental health
  - Providing assistance to those who cannot otherwise access it.

Student Survey

Ten of the students who participated in the survey were from the April 2022 to July 2022 course offered in Maryland. Two were from the January 2019 to May 2019 course offered in Hawaii. Three students participated in the survey from the January 2018 to May 2018 course offered in England. The students who participated from Maryland were given the survey at the conclusion of the final class under the supervision of the instructor. The survey

Case Studies

sought to determine what the students learned in the course about their own anxiety and depression and how they have learned to work through anxiety and depression utilizing methods taught in the course. Each student was surveyed individually with a parent in the room.

Survey MD9M: Maryland, age 9, M

MD9M participated in the Kindness Project Spiritual Self-Care class from April 2022 to July 2022. MD9M is diagnosed with attention deficit hyperactivity disorder (ADHD) and generalized anxiety disorder (GAD). The students were only on medication when they began the course. Therapy is not currently covered by the guardian's insurance. The guardian has stated that toward the end of the sixteen weeks course the student set up a Zen Garden as a vigil in their bedroom and seems to be having fewer disciplinary actions required during the day.

Interview Script with MD9M

Interviewer: Can you draw for me what anxiety looks like for you?

Notes: Students drew a monster hidden in a shadow. Interviewer notes that the monster is larger in comparison to the self-portrait of the picture.

Interviewer: How often do you feel anxious?

MD9M: "Whenever I do something wrong but don't mean to. I feel anxious that I am going to get in trouble. I also worry about going to school next year. I already have a bad reputation."

Interviewer: Understandable. Do you think there are things you learned this summer that can help with going back to school? Would you mind writing or drawing your answer under "I work through my anxiety by . . ."

Notes: MD9M wrote the word "breath" on the worksheet.

Interviewer: Can you tell me more about that word?

MD9M: "I liked learning to control my breathing. I think it helps."

Interviewer: Can you draw for me what depression looks like?

Notes: MD9M drew a self-portrait with half their body in the shadows

Interviewer: Can you tell me a little bit about this picture?

MD9M: "I think depression feels like hiding."

Notes: Guardian interjects at this point to mention that this is the first time MD9C has expressed having felt depression before.

Interviewer: Can you draw or write how you work through your depression?

Notes: MD9M wrote the word "living."

Interviewer: Can you tell me a little bit more about what this word means?

MD9M: "I just keep living. That's how I win."

Interviewer: On this last page, can you draw or write what your favorite form of spiritual self-care is?

Notes: Student wrote the words "Zen Garden."

Interviewer: Do you remember which class this was taught in?

MD9M: "Vigil Meditation."

Final Notes: Student MD9C first came to the program with obvious behavioral problems. Initial interactions were disruptive and attention seeking. By the conclusion of the course, the student was interacting objectively in the lessons.

Case Studies

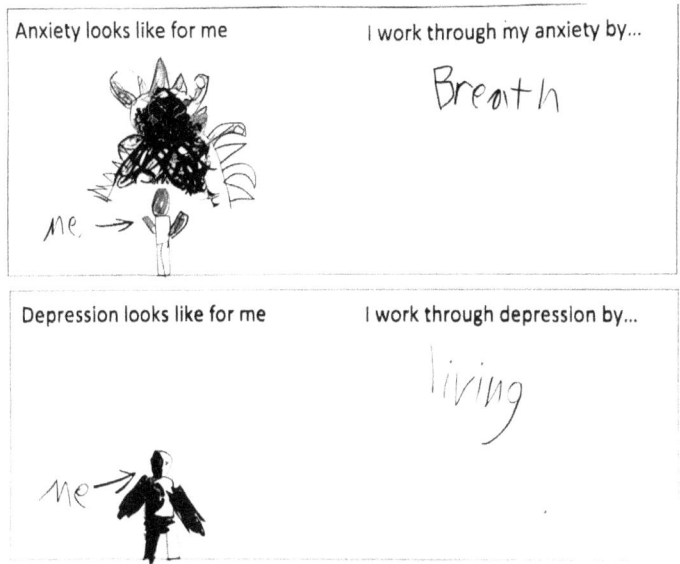

My favorite form of Spiritual Self-Care that I learned in this class is....

Survey MD10F: Maryland, age 10, Female

MD10F participated in the Kindness Project Spiritual Self-Care class from April 2022 to July 2022. MD10F is not currently diagnosed with any mental health disorders. MD10F was consistently interactive throughout the course, asked relevant questions, and engaged in all of the material. The student seemed excited to be learning new skills.

Interview Script with MD10F

Interviewer: Can you draw for me what anxiety looks like for you?

Notes: MD10F colored the entire block in with a black crayon.

Interviewer: How often do you feel anxious?

MD10F: "Pretty much every day. I am worried about school next year. I start middle school."

Interviewer: Starting in a new school can be very stressful. Do you think there are things you learned this summer that can help with going to a new school? Would you mind writing or drawing your answer under "I work through my anxiety by . . ."

Notes: MD10F drew a light switch flipped on.

Interviewer: Can you tell me more about that picture?

MD10F: "My anxiety feels like darkness. Sometimes when I feel anxious, I can turn the light on by doing things you taught me."

Interviewer: Can you draw for me what depression looks like?

Notes: Student drew a stick person standing next to a circled star.

Interviewer: Can you tell me a little bit about this picture?

MD9C: "I read that this star stands for evil things and depression feels evil."

Notes: Student noted a symbol from a different religion as being evil; the interviewer does not share this viewpoint but felt this interview was not the time or place to discuss this topic. The

Case Studies

interviewer also notes that the stick figure in the drawing appears to be smiling.

Interviewer: I noticed the stick figure is smiling, can you tell me why?

MD10F: "Sometimes I smile even when I am depressed."

Interviewer: Can you draw or write how you work through your depression?

Notes: Student drew the circled star symbol in purple and crossed out in yellow.

Interviewer: Can you explain the picture you drew to me?

MD10F: "The yellow is happy thoughts, and it is crossing out the evil."

Interviewer: On this last page, can you draw or write what your favorite form of spiritual self-care is?

Notes: Student drew stick figures walking with a pencil and a stick figure laying down.

Interviewer: Can you explain this picture to me?

MD10F: "It's a picture of when we went forest bathing. I think being outside helps me the best."

Final Notes: MD10F is going into sixth grade and came into the program with very little knowledge on anxiety or depression.

Trust Their Struggle

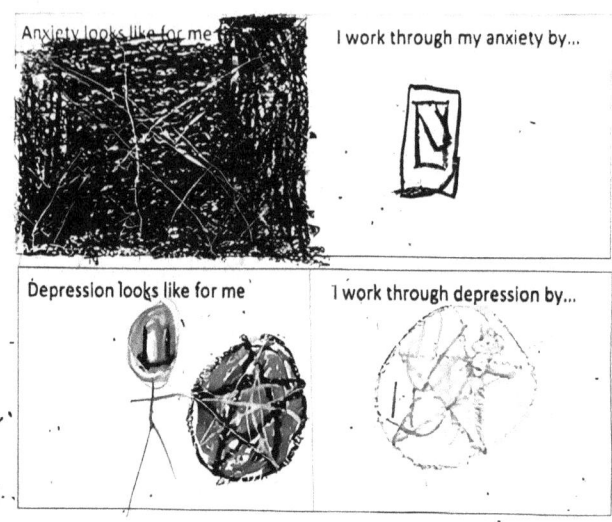

My favorite form of Spiritual Self-Care that I learned in this class is....

Case Studies

Survey MD7M: Maryland, age 7, Male

MD7M has been diagnosed with generalized anxiety disorder (GAD) and sensory processing disorder (SPD). MD7M is currently being evaluated for autism spectrum disorder (ASD). When the student began the course, he was quiet and chose not to interact with other students or in the initial activities. By the end of the sixteen-week course the student was fully engaged in each lesson.

Interview Script with MD7M

Interviewer: Can you draw for me what anxiety looks like for you?

Notes: Student drew a stick figure with various objects sticking out of their head and other body parts.

Interviewer: Can you explain this picture to me?

MD7M: "I think that when I am anxious it hurts sometimes, and I feel like I am being judged. So, this is me as a bug."

Notes: The personification of the bug in association with anxiety might indicate feeling vulnerable and unsafe.

Interviewer: Sometimes when we feel anxious, we also feel unsafe. It's okay to feel this way. Can you draw for me how you work through your anxiety when it comes up?

Notes: Student drew a picture of a person standing between two lines with what looks like a speaker crossed out on one side.

Interviewer: Can you explain this picture to me?

MD7M: "It helps when I hide from noise and sit alone for a minute and breathe through it."

Notes: Student is describing a sensory canceling room.

Interviewer: Can you draw for me what depression looks like?

Notes: Student drew a person who appears angry, standing under a dark circle.

Interviewer: Can you tell me a little bit about this picture?

Trust Their Struggle

MD7M: "This is me standing under a dark cloud, and it's raining."

Interviewer: Can you draw or write how you work through your depression?

Notes: Student drew a picture of a person in bed without the light on.

Interviewer: Can you explain the picture you drew to me?

MD7M: "When I feel scared or anxious or depressed, I like to be alone without anything on. Then I feel safe again."

Notes: Since MD7M suffers from SPD, it makes perfect sense that eliminating sensory objects or interactions would have a calming effect.

Interviewer: On this last page, can you draw or write what your favorite form of spiritual self-care is?

Notes: Student drew a picture of a box with three sections on it.

Interviewer: Can you explain this picture to me?

MD7M: "I like to journal. My mom got me a new journal so I can draw how I am feeling and let God know too. This was my favorite lesson."

Final Notes: MD7M is reacting to the different aspects of the program in a very appropriate way for his diagnosis. He consistently demonstrates a theme of needing time away from high sensory situations in order to process his emotions. This student also demonstrated a strong interest in faith and developing a relationship with God throughout the program.

Case Studies

My favorite form of Spiritual Self-Care that I learned in this class is....

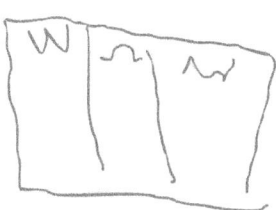

Survey MD5M: Maryland, age 5, Male

MD5M is the youngest participant in the Maryland class. He does not currently have any mental health diagnosis and is taking the course with his non-binary sibling. Their mother is a pediatric mental health therapist.

Interview Script with MD5M

Interviewer: Can you draw for me what anxiety looks like for you?

Notes: Student drew a series of shapes.

Interviewer: Can you explain this picture to me?

MD5M: "This is a picture of me when my mom lets the dogs outside without a leash."

Notes: Interviewer recognizes that at this age anxiety is less abstract and is more likely to be associated with specific situations.

Interviewer: Can you draw for me what you do to calm down when your mom lets the dogs off their leash?

Notes: Interviewer is adjusting the questions to be more specific due to the age of the participant. The student drew a stick figure laying down.

Interviewer: Can you explain this picture to me?

MD5M: "This is me laying on the couch and breathing, like this..." (Student proceeds to demonstrate deep breathing exercises) "and this (points to the stick figure standing up) is me when I'm done because I feel better."

Interviewer: Can you draw for me what depression looks like?

Notes: Student draws two stick figures and then crosses one out.

Interviewer: Can you tell me a little bit about this picture?

MD5M: "This one is me (points to the non-crossed out picture) and this one is my friends leaving school." (Points to the crossed-out picture)

Case Studies

Notes: Student has again interpreted the feeling of depression with a specific event.

Interviewer: It can be really sad when our friends have to go home, and we can't go with them. Can you draw what you do when your friends go home that makes you feel better?

Notes: The interviewer changed the structure of the question in order to meet the intellectual level of the student. Students drew several stick figures; some appear to be hugging.

Interviewer: Can you explain the picture you drew to me?

MD5M: "When my friends go home, I play with my brother and sister and mom and dad and then I am happy again."

Interviewer: On this last page, can you draw an activity or game that you learned in this class was?

Notes: Student drew a smiling stick figure who appears to be seated.

Interviewer: Can you explain this picture to me?

MD5M: "This is me meditating."

Final Notes: MD5M is registered to attend the next sixteen-week session. He has demonstrated a willingness to learn and be included in the activities and lessons with the other kids. He has a basic understanding of what events to associate with depression and anxiety.

Trust Their Struggle

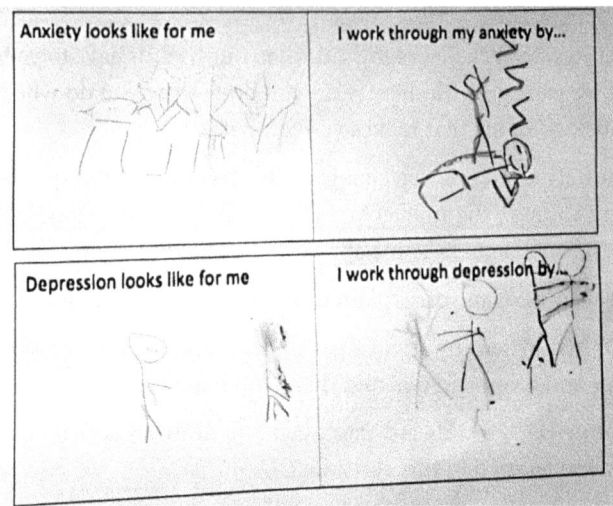

My favorite form of Spiritual Self-Care that I learned in this class is....

Case Studies

Assessments, Evaluations, and Conclusions

There is a difference between suicide prevention and suicide intervention. Intervention practices are implemented after a child or youth has been diagnosed as needing services. Prevention is implemented long before intervention is ever necessary. There is no one-size-fits-all solution to suicide prevention. The Kindness Project was designed with this in mind. The program educates children and youth on different methods of coping with stress, anxiety, and depression, with the added implementation of learning to utilize these practices to connect with the divine.

Not every child will find the Kindness Project to be helpful or relatable. However, the human subject study did demonstrate positive results in the lives of those who participated in the program. The children and youth who participated in the program came out of the program with a better understanding of what anxiety and depression are and how to cope with these disorders. Several of the children who were interviewed provided insight into how the program was helping them in their everyday lives. The older students indicated a decrease in stress over homework, chores, and social events. The younger students found they enjoyed spending time on their own and working through problems through crafts and internal engagement.

Many of the parents whose children participated in the program saw an improvement in behavior as well. Most indicated that this improvement was not isolated to the home environment but in school and other social activities as well. Most expressed that their children continued to practice the activities they learned long after they completed the program. In a continuation study, there may be interest in interviewing the educators of the students involved in the program to determine behavioral differences in the classroom following participation in the Kindness Project.

The key conclusion from the study is that this program provides an easily implementable curriculum for churches and other faiths to follow with little to no educational requirements of the facilitators. The purpose of the program was to provide churches with a way to be part of the solution in suicide prevention without requiring a large budget or higher education. I believe that this human subject study demonstrates success in these goals within this program.

5

Practical Exercise Workbook

I can do all things through him who strengthens me.
—Phil 4:13

Week—Topics Discussed

1. Discuss different Bible stories where Jesus and/or his disciples practiced self-care.
2. What is self-care? What is spiritual self-care? How are they different? How are they the same?
3. What is mental health? What are stress and anxiety? How does mental health relate to self-care?
4. What is mental health? What is depression? How does self-care relate to depression?
5. What is a trigger? Can you identify triggers in your own life? Complete a worksheet on trigger identification and current reaction.
6. What is grounding? How do we ground ourselves? When do we use grounding?

7. Conversational Prayer. What is it? How to practice it? Practical application.
8. Devotional Meditation. What is it? How to practice it? Practical application.
9. Vigil Meditation. What is it? How to practice it? Practical application.
10. Forest Bathing. What is it? How to practice it? Practical application.
11. Creative Spirituality. What is it? How to practice it? Practical application. (Art)
12. Creative Spirituality. What is it? How to practice it? Practical application. (Movement)
13. Creative Spirituality. What is it? How to practice it? Practical application. (Written)
14. Christian Yoga Meditation. What is it? How to practice it? Practical application.
15. Active Listening. What is it? How to practice it? Practical application.
16. Mantra Practice. What is it? How to practice it? Practical application.
17. Developing your own spiritual self-care plan. Students will engage in everything they have learned over the past several weeks and create a plan of action for their own spiritual self-care.

Lesson 1: Jesus and Self-Care

Note to leader: this meeting should be no more than 1.5 hours. The point of this program is to educate but not to overwhelm.

Before the Meeting

If providing mats, place them on the floor with enough space between each one for each youth to reach their arms out without touching anyone else. If the youth are bringing their own mats, use brightly colored tape to denote spaces where their mats can be placed on the floor to ensure proper spacing.

Also, set up the gathering game. Place blank white paper on the wall or on a table. This can be a large piece of paper or several small printer-sized sheets of paper. Lay out the markers as well.

Be sure to have the following items on hand:

Bible

Floor mats (if providing them)

White Paper

Markers

Matt 22:36–39; Luke 2:46, 5:16; John 6:11; Mark 1:35, 6:30–32, bookmarked.

Gathering (5–10 min)

As the students arrive, have them go over to the table and draw a picture of what they believe self-care looks like. Older students can write words instead of drawing a picture. Once finished, have the students take a seat on a mat on the floor. If they drew on a personal piece of paper, they could take it back to their mat with them.

Opening (10 min)

At this point everyone should be back in their seats. Ask each student to share what they drew or wrote. Open with your own drawing first and then say we will go around the room. Have students explain why this is self-care for them.

Opening Prayer (2 min)

"May we be blessed today by Your presence, Lord. May we understand more about Your Word and how we should conduct self-care. May You lift each of us up in You. Amen." (You can change the prayer to match your denomination or faith.)

Lesson Bible Story

Mark 12:30

> And you shall love the Lord your God with all your heart and with all your soul and with all your mind and with all your strength.'

Say: "The cornerstone of the Kindness Project is this verse. In this verse Jesus calls us to love our neighbors as we love ourselves. Therefore, if we do not love ourselves, we cannot love our neighbors. Spiritual self-care helps us to connect to God on a deeper level, and through these methods, Jesus guides us to self-love."

The Lesson (30–40 min)

Have the students stand in a circle.

Say: "I am going to read a quick Bible verse at the start of each round. I will then say the different ways that Jesus practiced self-care in that verse. If you also do this to practice self-care, walk into the circle and take the spot of someone else who came out of the circle. For example, if I say he prayed, everyone who prays should walk into the center of the circle and then take a new spot in the circle. Once you take a new spot, introduce yourself to the person next to you."

Do a quick demonstration of the game by saying "Jesus prayed" and walk into the center of the circle. Then go stand on the opposite side. There is an option to use a parachute and have the kids run underneath it to add a new fun element.

For each verse, the examples can be:

Luke 2:46
Jesus asked for help
Jesus learned new things

John 6:11
Jesus showed gratitude (Jesus was grateful)
Jesus ate healthily

Mark 1:35
Jesus went for a walk
Jesus prayed
Jesus meditated

Mark 6:30–32
Jesus rested
Jesus sat alone

Luke 5:16
Jesus prayed alone
Jesus walked alone

To close out the game have the students find their mats. Review the different ways Jesus practiced self-care.

Positive Affirmation (2–5 min)

This is the only part of the class that is not challenge-by-choice. Every student must participate.

Have the students go around the room and say one positive thing about themselves. This can be anything from something they like about their appearance to something they are good at. Follow this statement "and I love myself." The key is specificity. The comment cannot be generic.

Example: "I have beautiful eyes, and I love myself."

Closing (5–10 min)

Have the students find a comfortable position to be in. This can be a laying down position. Tell the kids to breath as deeply as they can in, and then breath as deeply as they can out. Have them do this two or three times with their eyes closed.

Meditation Script for the Week

Continue to breathe in (take a deep breath) *and out* (exhale).

As I count down from 5, I want you to picture your body sinking into the ground in the same way you sink into your bed.

5... You relax your head and shoulders into your mat (take a deep breath in and out).

4... You relax your neck and arms into your mat (take a deep breath in and out).

3... You relax your hands and stomach, focusing on your breathing (take a deep breath in and out).

2 . . . You relax your legs and feet into your mat (take a deep breath in and out)

1 . . . You feel yourself drift into your safe space

In this space I want you to picture your perfect space. (Take a deep breath in and out.)

This space is entirely your own. This can be a trail in the forest, a swimming hole in the ocean, a corner of your bedroom, in front of a fireplace on a camping trip, in a gaming community online, or any other place you can think of. (Take a deep breath in and out.)

In this space, I want you to acknowledge the feeling this space gives you. Understand that you can be whoever God made you to be in this space. Safe. Secure. If your imagination wanders away from your safe space, focus back on your breathing and when you are ready, head back into your space.

Now sit in this space for the next few minutes. Enjoy this time in your safe space. (Wait no less than two minutes in silence or with light music playing.)

Now I am going to count you back home.

5 . . . You start to move away from your safe space and focus back on your breathing.

4 . . . You start to wiggle your fingers, feeling the mat beneath you.

3 . . . You start to wiggle your toes, focus on your breathing.

2 . . . You bring awareness back to your whole self and open your eyes.

1 . . . When you are ready, you can sit up.

Then pray: "Lord, thank you for bringing us all together today in this space. We pray for each person in this room and their mental health. May you guide them to a place of peace, until we meet again."

Lesson 2: What is Self-Care/Spiritual Self-Care

Note to leader: this meeting should be no more than 1.5 hours. The point of this program is to educate but not to overwhelm.

Before the Meeting

If providing mats, place them on the floor with enough space between each one for each youth to reach their arms out without touching anyone else. If the youth are bringing their own mats, use brightly colored tape to denote spaces where their mats can be placed on the floor to ensure proper spacing.

Set up the gathering game. Write the following words on pieces of note cards (feel free to add new ones as needed or wanted):

Healthy eating

Silent hikes

Meditation

Prayer

Breathing exercises

Journaling

Reading

Silent coloring

Mindfulness

Sleeping

Bathing

Yoga

Place all the self-care notecards on the table in a pile. On another space on the table, place two labels. One says "Spiritual Self-Care" and the other says "Regular Self-Care."

Be sure to have the following items on hand:

Bible

Floor mats (if providing them)

Self-care note cards and labels

Gathering (5–10 min)

As the students arrive, after they have laid out their mat or chosen a mat, have them migrate over to the tables. They must work together to determine which note card goes into which category. Is the card regular self-care, or is it self-care for the soul?

Opening (10 min)

Once they are satisfied with their decision, pick up one card at a time and ask the students to explain why they felt it went in one category and not the other. Don't correct them. Just actively listen to their thoughts on the subject.

Opening Prayer (2 min)

"Lord, thank you for this time together. As we move through today's lesson on the difference between self-care and spiritual self-care, I hope you will be with us and guide us toward your wisdom and light. Amen."

Trust Their Struggle

The Lesson (30 min)

The teacher: "Can anyone tell me the difference between self-care and spiritual care?"

Let the students answer.

The teacher: "Self-care, whether spiritual or not, is important for helping with stress, anxiety, and big emotions. Regular self-care keeps us healthy physically, but spiritual self-care keeps us healthy emotionally and mentally."

Take the cards and put them into a new pile. Ask for a volunteer to come up and act out one of the cards.

The Game

Have the student act out the self-care on the card. The rest of the students must guess what the card says AND whether it's spiritual or regular. Some forms of self-care are both. Talk about why each card falls into each category.

Teacher Cheat Sheet

Healthy eating: Regular self-care. This form of self-care is great for the body but doesn't dig deeper than healthy habits.

Silent hikes: Spiritual self-care. This form of self-care gives the person an opportunity to be alone with their thoughts and with Jesus.

Meditation: Spiritual self-care. This form of self-care gives the person an opportunity to be alone with their thoughts and with Jesus.

Prayer: Spiritual self-care. This form of self-care gives the person an opportunity to be alone with their thoughts and with Jesus.

Breathing exercises: Spiritual self-care. This form of self-care focuses on digging deeper into ourselves in order to form a sense of calm.

Journaling: Spiritual self-care. This form of self-care gives the person an opportunity to be alone with their thoughts and with Jesus.

Reading: Regular self-care. This form of self-care is great for the mind but doesn't dig deeper than healthy habits. However, reading can be combined with a spiritual form of self-care to help guide the spiritual self-care experience to go in a different direction

Silent coloring: Spiritual self-care. This form of self-care gives the person an opportunity to be alone with their thoughts and with Jesus.

Mindfulness: Spiritual self-care. This form of self-care gives the person an opportunity to be alone with their thoughts and with Jesus.

Sleeping: Regular self-care. This form of self-care is great for the mind and body but doesn't dig deeper than healthy habits.

Bathing: Regular self-care. This form of self-care is great for the body but doesn't dig deeper than healthy habits.

Yoga: Spiritual Self-care. This form of self-care gives the person an opportunity to be alone with their thoughts and with Jesus.

Positive Affirmation (2–5 min)

This is the only part of the class that is not challenge by choice. Every student must participate.

Have the students go around the room and say one positive thing about themselves. This can be anything from something they like about their appearance to something they are good at. Follow this statement by "and I love myself." They key is specificity. The comment cannot be generic.

Example: "I have beautiful eyes, and I love myself."

Closing

Have the students find a comfortable position to be in. This can be a laying down position. Tell the kids to breath as deeply as they can in, and then breath as deeply as they can out. Have them do this two or three times with their eyes closed.

Meditation Script for the Week

Continue to breathe in (take a deep breath) *and out* (exhale).

As I count down from 5, I want you to picture your body sinking into the ground in the same way you sink into your bed.

5 . . . You relax your head and shoulders into your mat (take a deep breath in and out).

4 . . . You relax your neck and arms into your mat (take a deep breath in and out).

3 . . . You relax your hands and stomach, focusing on your breathing (take a deep breath in and out).

2 . . . You relax your legs and feet into your mat (take a deep breath in and out).

1 . . . You feel yourself drift into your safe space.

In this space I want you to picture your perfect space. (Take a deep breath in and out)

This space is entirely your own. This can be a trail in the forest, a swimming hole in the ocean, a corner of your bedroom, in front of a fireplace on a camping trip, in a gaming community online, or any other place you can think of. (Take a deep breath in and out.)

In this space, I want you to acknowledge the feeling this space gives you. Understand that you can be whoever God made you to be in this space. Safe. Secure. If your imagination wanders away from your safe space, focus back on your breathing, and when you are ready, head back into your space.

Now sit in this space for the next few minutes. Enjoy this time in your safe space. (Wait no less than 2 minutes in silence or with light music playing)

Now I am going to count you back home.

5 . . . You start to move away from your safe space and focus back on your breathing.

4 . . . You start to wiggle your fingers, feeling the mat beneath you.

3 . . . You start to wiggle your toes, focus on your breathing.

2 . . . You bring awareness back to your whole self and open your eyes.

1 . . . When you are ready, you can sit up.

Then pray: "Lord, thank you for bringing us all together today in this space. We pray for each person in this room and their mental health. May you guide them to a place of peace, until we meet again."

Lesson 3: What is Stress and Anxiety?

Note to leader: this meeting should be no more than 1.5 hours. The point of this program is to educate but not to overwhelm

Before the Meeting

If providing mats, place them on the floor with enough space between each one for each youth to reach their arms out without touching anyone else. If the youth are bringing their own mats, use brightly colored tape to denote spaces where their mats can be placed on the floor to ensure proper spacing.

This week we will dive into emotions and feelings. Be ready to actively listen to your students' stories. If they are having trouble opening up, be ready with a story of your own to help them feel more comfortable sharing.

Set up the gathering game. Around the room hang up poster board with one word of the following words on each poster:

Anxiety

Sadness

Anger

Fear

Stress

Leave markers at the front of the room.

Be sure to have the following items on hand:

Bible

Floor mats (if providing them)

6 Poster Boards

Markers

Worksheet Packets (1 per child)

Gathering (5–10 min)

As the students arrive have them go around the room and mark each poster board with whatever words come to mind when they read the words already on the board. There are no wrong answers. Even silly ones are welcome, as they break up the tension in the room. You can even start by writing a small word on each board to demonstrate.

Ask the students to take their seats as they finish up.

If working with younger children, instead of using poster boards, have them come in and stand in front of the word that they remember feeling before. When working with five- to nine-year-olds some of these words won't mean much to them, so just reading them out loud and letting them choose an emotion they've felt before will help engage them in this lesson.

Opening (20 min)

Go around the room and have each student share something they wrote on the wall. If working with younger kids, ask them to tell you a story about a time they felt that emotion.

Once everyone has shared, thank them for sharing and have them return to their mats.

Opening Prayer (2 min)

"May we be blessed today by Your presence, Lord. May we understand more about Your Word and how we should conduct self-care. May You lift each of us up in You. Amen." (You can change the prayer to match your denomination or faith.)

Lesson Bible Story: Luke 4:1–14

Read:

> Jesus, full of the Holy Spirit, left the Jordan and was led by the Spirit into the wilderness, where for forty days he was tempted by the devil. He ate nothing during those days, and at the end of them he was hungry. The devil said to him, "If you are the Son of God, tell this stone to become bread." Jesus answered, "It is written: 'Man shall not live on bread alone.'" The devil led him up to a high place and showed him in an instant all the kingdoms of the world. And he said to him, "I will give you all their authority and splendor; it has been given to me, and I can give it to anyone I want to. If you worship me, it will all be yours." Jesus answered, "It is written: 'Worship the Lord your God and serve him only.'" The devil led him to Jerusalem and had him stand on the highest point of the temple. "If you are the Son of God," he said, "throw yourself down from here. For it is written: '"He will command his angels concerning you to guard you carefully; they will lift you up in their hands, so that you will not strike your foot against a stone."' Jesus answered, "It is said: 'Do not put the Lord your God to the test.'" When the devil had finished all this tempting, he left him until an opportune time. Jesus returned to Galilee in the power of the Spirit, and news about him spread through the whole countryside.

Discussion

What are some symptoms of stress or anxiety that Jesus showed in this story?

Answer: Not eating. Isolation. Over-exercising. Putting self in dangerous situations.

In this verse Jesus is being led and tempted by Satan to deny his Father. While we know Jesus is the Son of God. We also know he was part human. In his humanity it is easy to understand that temptation from Satan can be stressful and can cause anxiety. Jesus responds by leaning closer into his Father and taking time to purposefully remove counteract Satan.

The Lesson (30–40 min)

Worksheet

Teacher: "Today we are going to talk about mental health. We are going to go over a few worksheets together."

Hand out the worksheets. The worksheets are attached to this lesson plan and are designed for every age group. If the younger ones cannot write words, they can respond with pictures. It is only important that they know what they drew. Follow the following prompt while working through the worksheet.

The first block asks the student to describe how they feel when stressed.

First, say, "Can anyone tell me what stress is?"

Let the students answer. Then say, "That's very good. Stress is when we experience something that is overwhelming, and we react negatively to it." Have the students draw or write in the block words that describe stress for them. There are no wrong answers.

Have the students then fill out the block that asks, describe a situation when you felt stressed. Ask if anyone would like to share. If not, this is okay. This is challenge by choice.

Next say, "Can anyone tell me what anxiety is?"

Let the students answer. Then say, "That's very good. Anxiety is when we experience when we experience uneasiness, stress, or dread about something we experience." Have the students draw or write in the block words that describe anxiety for them. There are no wrong answers.

Have the students then fill out the block that asks, describe a situation when you felt anxious. Ask if anyone would like to share. If not, this is okay. This is challenge by choice.

Then say, "Can anyone tell me the difference between stress and anxiety?"

Let the students answer. Then say, "The biggest difference between stress and anxiety is the length and severity of the reaction. Anxiety will last longer and have more severe reactions than stress will."

Play the Anxiety-Safe Space game.

Game: Anxiety and Safe Space

For this game, the teacher selects one or two students to be "Anxiety." Anxiety stands in the middle of the room or field. Everyone else stands on one end of the field. The teacher designates one area on each side of the room or field as a safe space. This can be a bench, tree, wall, etc. The object of the game is for students to get from one safe space to the other without getting tagged by Anxiety. If they are tagged, they join the Anxiety students in the center. Students spend ten seconds in the safe space and then have to run back across the field to the other safe space.

Refer to the model below for an explanation. Play several rounds. At the completion of the game discuss how safe spaces can be helpful in combating anxiety. Go back to the final part of the worksheet.

Practical Exercise Workbook

Worksheet

Ask the students to fill out the next two blocks. Describe your safe space and describe your safety person. These two are completely individual. The safe space can be a real place, a video game world, or a completely made-up place they go in their head to get away. The safety person should be someone they feel comfortable talking

Trust Their Struggle

to when they feel stressed or anxious. For any child who is struggling to answer either of these, be ready with examples such as family members, their favorite spot in their house, the church, etc.

Positive Affirmation (2–5 min)

This is the only part of the class that is not challenge by choice. Every student must participate.

Have the students go around the room and say one positive thing about themselves. This can be anything from something they like about their appearance to something they are good at. Follow this statement by "and I love myself." They key is specificity. The comment cannot be generic.

Example: "I have beautiful eyes, and I love myself."

Closing

Have the students find a comfortable position to be in. This can be a laying down position. Tell the kids to breath as deeply as they can in, and then breath as deeply as they can out. Have them do this two or three times with their eyes closed.

Meditation Script for the Week

Continue to breathe in (take a deep breath) *and out* (exhale).

As I count down from 5, I want you to picture your body sinking into the ground in the same way you sink into your bed.

5 . . . You relax your head and shoulders into your mat (take a deep breath in and out)

4 . . . You relax your neck and arms into your mat (take a deep breath in and out)

3 . . . You relax your hands and stomach, focusing on your breathing (take a deep breath in and out)

2 . . . You relax your legs and feet into your mat (take a deep breath in and out)

1 . . . You feel yourself drift into your safe space

In this space I want you to picture your perfect space. (Take a deep breath in and out)

This space is entirely your own. This can be a trail in the forest, a swimming hole in the ocean, a corner of your bedroom, in front of a fireplace on a camping trip, in a gaming community online, or any other place you can think of. (Take a deep breath in and out)

In this space, I want you to acknowledge the feeling this space gives you. Understand that you can be whoever God made you to be in this space. Safe. Secure. If your imagination wanders away from your safe space, focus back on your breathing and when you are ready, head back into your space.

Now sit in this space for the next few minutes. Enjoy this time in your safe space. (Wait no less than two minutes in silence or with light music playing)

Now I am going to count you back home.

5 . . . You start to move away from your safe space and focus back on your breathing

4 . . . You start to wiggle your fingers, feeling the mat beneath you

3 . . . You start to wiggle your toes, focus on your breathing

2 . . . You bring awareness back to your whole self and open your eyes

1 . . . When you are ready, you can sit up

Then pray: "Lord, thank you for bringing us all together today in this space. We pray for each person in this room and their mental health. May you guide them to a place of peace, until we meet again."

Trust Their Struggle

Describe how you feel when stressed	Describe how you feel when anxious
Describe a situation when you feel stressed	Describe a situation when you feel anxious

PLAY THE ANXIETY GAME

Describe your safe space	Describe your safety person

Lesson 4: What is Depression?

Note to leader: this meeting should be no more than 1.5 hours. The point of this program is to educate but not to overwhelm.

Before the Meeting

If providing mats, place them on the floor with enough space between each one for each youth to reach their arms out without touching anyone else. If the youth are bringing their own mats, use brightly colored tape to denote spaces where their mats can be placed on the floor to ensure proper spacing.

Set up the gathering activity. Place worksheet 1 (provided in this packet) on the ground in front of each students mat with a packet of markers or crayons.

Be sure to have the following items on hand:

Bible

Floor mats (if providing them)

Worksheets included in this packet

Markers/crayons

Two balls (soccer balls work well)

Trust Their Struggle

Gathering (5–10 min)

As the students arrive have them draw on their worksheet what they think they look like when they are very sad. If they are older, you can use the term Depressed.

Opening: (10 min)

When the students begin to finish their worksheets, ask if they would like to share what they drew. As students are sharing, take note of the individuals who have an easier time describing depression or sadness. Some students will have experienced depression on a deeper level then others.

Opening Prayer (2 min)

"May we be blessed today by Your presence, Lord. May we understand more about Your Word and how we should conduct self-care. May You lift each of us up in You. Amen." (You can change the prayer to match your denomination or faith.)

Lesson Bible Story: Hab 3:16–19

> I hear, and my body trembles.
> at the sound, my lips quiver.
> Decay invades my bones,
> my legs tremble beneath me.
> I await the day of distress
> that will come upon the people who attack us.
> For though the fig tree does not blossom,
> and no fruit appears on the vine,
> Though the yield of the olive fails
> and the terraces produce no nourishment,
> Though the flocks disappear from the fold
> and there is no herd in the stalls,

Practical Exercise Workbook

> Yet I will rejoice in the Lord
> and exult in my saving God.
> God, my Lord, is my strength.
> he makes my feet swift as those of deer
> and enables me to tread upon the heights.

Discussion:

Question: What do you think are some symptoms of depression talked about in this verse?

Answer: In the first portion of this verse, the individual is talking about hopelessness and a deep sense of sadness. He describes events happening around him that are causing him stress and anxiety. It is important to realize that continued exposure to events that cause stress or anxiety can lead to depression.

In the verse this individual is experiencing depression and is holding on to the hope that the Lord provides to anchor him to the earth despite feeling lost and hopeless. In many ways this verse is showing us how important it is to lean on God for our own hope.

The Lesson

Worksheet

Teacher: "Today I want to go over depression. Can anyone tell me what depression is?"

While the students are answering, hand out the second worksheet.

Teacher: "Depression is a persistent sadness and a lack of interest or pleasure in previously rewarding or enjoyable activities. Does anyone want to share a time they felt depressed? Has anyone ever felt hopelessness like the man in our verse for the day?"

Let students respond, then ask the students to turn to their worksheets.

Trust Their Struggle

Go over each symptom of depression. Ask the students to circle any symptom they have experienced. Explain that these are not the only symptoms and encourage them to add their own if they wish.

Next ask the students to fill in the bottom block. The first block asks the student to describe a time they felt depressed, what was happening during that time in their lives? (i.e., new school, new baby in the family; it's okay for them to say nothing.) What were you doing that tells you that you were depressed?

Game

Have the students stand in a circle.

Rules:

Students softly toss the ball around the circle. In round one, students have to say one positive thing about themselves when they catch the ball. The student then throws it to a new person without saying their name or gaining their attention. If a student does not have the ball they should be watching the ball to ensure they are focused on the ball when it is thrown to them.

In round two, the teacher can introduce a second ball to the circle. This call will be lightly kicked around the circle. This is silent ball, so students should not be talking but rather focusing on the two balls. See how fast you can move the balls around the circle without talking.

Positive Affirmation (2–5 min)

This is the only part of the class that is not challenge by choice. Every student must participate.

Have the students go around the room and say one positive thing about themselves. This can be anything from something they like about their appearance to something they are good at. Follow this statement by "and I love myself." They key is specificity. The comment cannot be generic.

Example: "I have beautiful eyes, and I love myself."

Closing

Have the students find a comfortable position to be in. This can be a laying down position. Tell the kids to breath as deeply as they can in, and then breath as deeply as they can out. Have them do this two or three times with their eyes closed.

Meditation Script for the Week

Continue to breathe in (take a deep breath) *and out* (exhale).

As I count down from 5, I want you to picture your body sinking into the ground in the same way you sink into your bed.

5 . . . You relax your head and shoulders into your mat (take a deep breath in and out)

4 . . . You relax your neck and arms into your mat (take a deep breath in and out)

3 . . . You relax your hands and stomach, focusing on your breathing (take a deep breath in and out)

2 . . . You relax your legs and feet into your mat (take a deep breath in and out)

1 . . . You feel yourself drift into your safe space

In this space I want you to picture your perfect space. (Take a deep breath in and out)

This space is entirely your own. This can be a trail in the forest, a swimming hole in the ocean, a corner of your bedroom, in front of a fireplace on a camping trip, in a gaming community online, or any other place you can think of. (Take a deep breath in and out)

Trust Their Struggle

In this space, I want you to acknowledge the feeling this space gives you. Understand that you can be whoever God made you to be in this space. Safe. Secure. If your imagination wanders away from your safe space, focus back on your breathing, and when you are ready, head back into your space.

Now sit in this space for the next few minutes. Enjoy this time in your safe space. (Wait no less than two minutes in silence or with light music playing)

Now I am going to count you back home.

5 . . . You start to move away from your safe space and focus back on your breathing

4 . . . You start to wiggle your fingers, feeling the mat beneath you

3 . . . You start to wiggle your toes, focus on your breathing

2 . . . You bring awareness back to your whole self and open your eyes

1 . . . When you are ready, you can sit up

Then pray: "Lord, thank you for bringing us all together today in this space. We pray for each person in this room and their mental health. May you guide them to a place of peace, until we meet again."

Practical Exercise Workbook

What are some symptoms of depression that YOU experience? Circle all the ones you think apply.

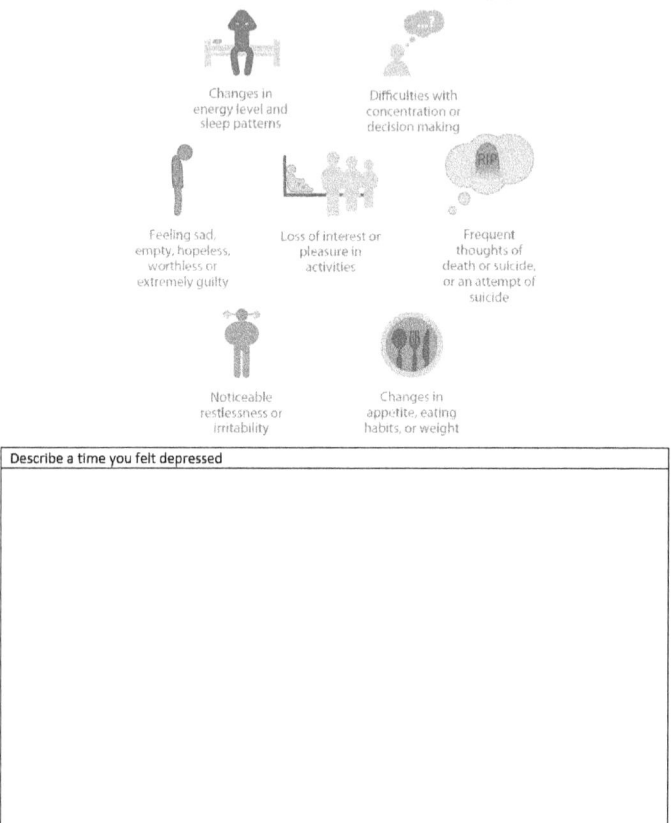

Changes in energy level and sleep patterns

Difficulties with concentration or decision making

Feeling sad, empty, hopeless, worthless or extremely guilty

Loss of interest or pleasure in activities

Frequent thoughts of death or suicide, or an attempt of suicide

Noticeable restlessness or irritability

Changes in appetite, eating habits, or weight

Describe a time you felt depressed

Lesson 5: Triggers

Note to leader: this meeting should be no more than 1.5 hours. The point of this program is to educate but not to overwhelm.

Before the Meeting

If providing mats, place them on the floor with enough space between each one for each youth to reach their arms out without touching anyone else. If the youth are bringing their own mats, use brightly colored tape to denote spaces where their mats can be placed on the floor to ensure proper spacing.

Set up the gathering activity. Place posters with pictures of triggering situations around the room.

Be sure to have the following items on hand:

Bible

Floor mats (if providing them)

Trigger Posters (printouts provided in this booklet)

Markers

Worksheet (printouts provided in this booklet)

Gathering (5–10 min)

As the students arrive, have the students find a poster that has a situation represented that made them feel upset or angry in the past. Ask them to either put a mark on the poster they relate to

Trust Their Struggle

or write their name. Once complete, have the students sit on their mats and wait for everyone else to finish.

Opening (10 min)

Walk around the room and talk about each triggering event. Ask the students to describe what is happening in the picture. Ask if anyone would like to share a time, they experienced this triggering event. You can open with your own story to help guide the conversation. Be sure to point out that multiple people in the room share similar triggering events.

Opening Prayer (2 min)

"May we be blessed today by Your presence, Lord. May we understand more about Your Word and how we should conduct self-care. May You lift each of us up in You. Amen." (You can change the prayer to match your denomination or faith.)

Lesson

Bible Story: Mark 11:12-19

> The next day as they were leaving Bethany, Jesus was hungry. Seeing in the distance a fig tree in leaf, he went to find out if it had any fruit. When he reached it, he found nothing but leaves, because it was not the season for figs. Then he said to the tree, "May no one ever eat fruit from you again." And his disciples heard him say it.
>
> On reaching Jerusalem, Jesus entered the temple courts and began driving out those who were buying and selling there. He overturned the tables of the money changers and the benches of those selling doves and would not allow anyone to carry merchandise through the temple

courts. And as he taught them, he said, "Is it not written: 'My house will be called a house of prayer for all nations'? But you have made it 'a den of robbers.'"

Discussion:

Question: What emotion was Jesus experiencing here?

Answer: Anger, Frustration.

Question: Can anyone tell me what may have triggered his anger?

Answer:

Jesus was hungry and there was no food immediately available.

There were people selling goods and using the temple as a marketplace rather than a place of worship or healing.

The Lesson (30–40 min)

Game

In this game, students will line up on one side of the room. The teacher will read off from the following list of triggers.

I felt excluded

I felt powerless

I felt unheard

I felt scolded

I felt judged

I felt blamed

I felt disrespected

I felt a lack of affection

I felt I couldn't speak up

I felt alone

I felt ignored

I felt I couldn't be honest

I felt like the bad guy

I felt forgotten

I felt unsafe

I felt unloved

I felt like something was unfair

I felt frustrated

I felt disconnected

I felt trapped

I felt a lack of passion

I felt uncared for

I felt manipulated

For every trigger read that a student relates to, they should take one step forward. Once all the triggers have been read, the students sit down where they are standing.

Question: Ask them why it is important to know what your triggers are. Let the students respond.

Answer: If we understand what our triggers are, we can take steps to prepare for or avoid those triggering situations.

Have students return to their mats.

Worksheet/Activity

Have students take a minute to complete the worksheet. Give examples for each block to help get students thinking.

Block 1: What can I do before a triggering event to help me through it?

Ideas: Meditate, talk to someone about how this event makes you feel

Block 2: What can I do during a triggering event to help me through it?

Ideas: Focus on my breathing, Excuse myself from the situation, set boundaries

Block 3: What can I do after a triggering event to help calm me down?

Ideas: Meditate, go for a walk, talk to someone

As students complete the worksheet ask if anyone wants to share their ideas.

Positive Affirmation (2–5 min)

This is the only part of the class that is not challenge by choice. Every student must participate.

Have the students go around the room and say one positive thing about themselves. This can be anything from something they like about their appearance to something they are good at. Follow this statement by "and I love myself." They key is specificity. The comment cannot be generic.

Example: "I have beautiful eyes, and I love myself."

Closing (5–10 min)

Have the students find a comfortable position to be in. This can be a laying down position. Tell the kids to breathe as deeply as they can in, and then breathe as deeply as they can out. Have them do these two or three times with their eyes closed.

Meditation Script for the Week

Continue to breathe in (take a deep breath) *and out* (exhale).

Trust Their Struggle

As I count down from 5, I want you to picture your body sinking into the ground in the same way you sink into your bed.

5 . . . You relax your head and shoulders into your mat (take a deep breath in and out)

4 . . . You relax your neck and arms into your mat (take a deep breath in and out)

3 . . . You relax your hands and stomach, focusing on your breathing (take a deep breath in and out)

2 . . . You relax your legs and feet into your mat (take a deep breath in and out)

1 . . . You feel yourself drift into your safe space

In this space I want you to picture your perfect space. (Take a deep breath in and out)

This space is entirely your own. This can be a trail in the forest, a swimming hole in the ocean, a corner of your bedroom, in front of a fireplace on a camping trip, in a gaming community online, or any other place you can think of. (Take a deep breath in and out)

In this space, I want you to acknowledge the feeling this space gives you. Understand that you can be whoever God made you to be in this space. Safe. Secure. If your imagination wanders away from your safe space, focus back on your breathing and when you are ready, head back into your space.

Now sit in this space for the next few minutes. Enjoy this time in your safe space. (Wait no less than two minutes in silence or with light music playing)

Now I am going to count you back home.

5 . . . You start to move away from your safe space and focus back on your breathing

4 . . . You start to wiggle your fingers, feeling the mat beneath you

3 . . . You start to wiggle your toes, focus on your breathing

2 . . . You bring awareness back to your whole self and open your eyes

Practical Exercise Workbook

1. . . *When you are ready, you can sit up*

Then pray: "Lord, thank you for bringing us all together today in this space. We pray for each person in this room and their mental health. May you guide them to a place of peace, until we meet again."

Trust Their Struggle

What can I do before a triggering event to help me through it?

What can I do during a triggering event to help me through it?

What can I do after a triggering event to help calm me down?

Lesson 6: Grounding

Note to leader: this meeting should be no more than 1.5 hours. The point of this program is to educate but not to overwhelm.

Before the Meeting

If providing mats, place them on the floor with enough space between each one for each youth to reach their arms out without touching anyone else. If the youth are bringing their own mats, use brightly colored tape to denote spaces where their mats can be placed on the floor to ensure proper spacing.

Set up the gathering activity.

Lay out attached Senses Countdown worksheet with crayons and pencils.

Gathering (5–10 min)

As students arrive have them take a worksheet and either write or draw in each block.

Opening (10 min)

Ask each student to share their Senses Countdown worksheet. Discuss how identifying physical items around you can help you find refocus when we experience a triggering event.

Opening Prayer (2 min)

"Lord, thank you for this time together. As we move through today's lesson on the grounding, I hope you will be with us and guide us toward your wisdom and light. Amen."

The Lesson (30 min)

Positive Affirmation (2–5 min)

This is the only part of the class that is not challenge by choice. Every student must participate.

Have the students go around the room and say one positive thing about themselves. This can be anything from something they like about their appearance to something they are good at. Follow this statement "and I love myself." The key is specificity. The comment cannot be generic.

Example: "I have beautiful eyes, and I love myself."

Activity (20–30 min)

This activity is best completed outside.

Ask: "What kind of hard feelings do we have today? Is anyone feeling angry, sad, or tired?"

Allow students time to share.

Say: "We are going to learn three ways that we can use to calm down when we are triggered. Does everyone remember what 'triggered' means?"

(If students need a reminder of last week's lesson, do a brief summary of what was learned.)

Have the students line up and walk thirty steps. Have them count the steps either out loud or in their head. Emphasize focusing on their steps. Once they have walked thirty steps, have them turn around and walk thirty steps back toward the start line.

Instruct the students to stand like a tree, tall with their arms out, and close their eyes when they get back to you.

Once all students are back and pretending to be a tree, have them breathe in while you count to four, then have them hold their breath while you count to two, then have them breathe out while you count to four.

Ex:

Breathe in: 1-2-3-4

Hold your breath: 1-2

Breathe out: 1-2-3-4

Ask: "How does everyone feel?"

Allow students to respond.

Discuss

"This is called grounding. Grounding is when we use elements of our environment to refocus us and to help keep us calm when we are triggered. Can anyone give me an example of when this might work for you?"

Allow students to answer.

Ask: "Is there a way we can alter these activities so we can use them when we are in a classroom or quiet setting?"

Allow students to answer.

Offer suggestions: "You can close your eyes at your desk or seat and do breathing exercises in your head. You can plant both feet on the ground, place both hands flat on your desk, and complete the five senses worksheet in your head. Even just closing your eyes and counting down from ten can be helpful.

Closing

Have the students find a comfortable position to be in. This can be a laying down position. Tell the kids to breathe as deeply as they can in, and then breathe as deeply as they can out. Have them do these two or three times with their eyes closed.

Continue to breathe in (take a deep breath) *and out* (exhale).

As I count down from 5, I want you to picture your body sinking into the ground in the same way you sink into your bed.

5 . . . You relax your head and shoulders into your mat (take a deep breath in and out)

4 . . . You relax your neck and arms into your mat (take a deep breath in and out)

3 . . . You relax your hands and stomach, focusing on your breathing (take a deep breath in and out)

2 . . . You relax your legs and feet into your mat (take a deep breath in and out)

1 . . . You feel yourself drift into your safe space

Imagine yourself as a tree.

If you are outside, you can take off your shoes to feel more connected with the earth.

Imagine your back as a trunk and that you have long roots that grow from the bottom of your feet, deep into the earth.

Grounding

You are standing in an open field with the sun shining down upon you. You are tall, strong, and solid.

Notice your feet in contact with the ground. Now feel them firmly anchored to the ground.

Practical Exercise Workbook

Now imagine strong roots extending from the bottoms of your feet, pushing downward through the surface below, eventually reaching into the soil below.

Feel your roots reaching even deeper into the earth, winding around rocks, and pushing deep through the many layers of cool, dark earth. Your roots grow and spread both downward and outward.

As you become more anchored, stretch your arms above your head, reach your tree-body, your trunk, straight and strong. Feel your leafy branches extend upward toward the warm sun. Wiggle your fingers; imagine your fingers are leaves blowing in a gentle wind.

As you are breathing, imagine with each exhale that you are pushing any tension or stress down toward your feet and out through your roots into the surrounding soil.

Feel tension draining from your eyes, your jaw, your shoulders, your chest, and your belly down into the earth.

When you feel properly grounded, take a deep breath, and reverse the process.

In this space, I want you to acknowledge the feeling this space gives you. Understand that you can be whoever God made you to be in this space. Safe. Secure. If your imagination wanders away from your safe space, focus back on your breathing and when you are ready, head back into your space.

Now sit in this space for the next few minutes. Enjoy this time in your safe space. (Wait no less than two minutes in silence or with light music playing)

Now I am going to count you back home.

5 . . . You start to move away from your safe space and focus back on your breathing

4 . . . You start to wiggle your fingers, feeling the mat beneath you

3 . . . You start to wiggle your toes, focus on your breathing

Trust Their Struggle

2 . . . You bring awareness back to your whole self and open your eyes

1 . . . When you are ready, you can sit up

Then pray: "Lord, thank you for bringing us all together today in this space. We pray for each person in this room and their mental health. May you guide them to a place of peace, until we meet again."

GROUNDING

5	Things you can see.	
4	Things you can touch.	
3	Things you can hear.	
2	Things you can smell.	
1	Thing you can taste.	

Lesson 7: Conversational Prayer

Note to leader: this meeting should be no more than 1.5 hours. The point of this program is to educate but not to overwhelm.

Before the Meeting

If providing mats, place them on the floor with enough space between each one for each youth to reach their arms out without touching anyone else. If the youth are bringing their own mats, use brightly colored tape to denote spaces where their mats can be placed on the floor to ensure proper spacing.

Set up the gathering game. Place three large pieces of paper on the wall. Label the first paper "What to pray for." Label the second paper "Prayed for." Label the third paper "God said." Place sticky notes on the table. Lay out the markers or crayons as well.

Be sure to have the following items on hand:

Bible

Floor mats (if providing them)

White Paper

Markers

Gathering (5–10 min)

As the students arrive have them take a sticky note and either draw a picture of or write something they would like prayed for today

Trust Their Struggle

and place it on the "What to pray for" poster. This can be anything they can think of.

Opening (10 min)

Once students are seated on their mat, ask if anyone would like to share what they wrote or drew on their sticky notes. Once everyone has shared, move on to the opening prayer. We will return to these boards in the lesson.

Opening Prayer (2 min)

"May we be blessed today by Your presence, Lord. May we understand more about Your Word and how we should conduct self-care. May You lift each of us up in You. Amen." (You can change the prayer to match your denomination or faith.)

Lesson Bible Story: John 11:38–44

> Jesus, once more deeply moved, came to the tomb. It was a cave with a stone laid across the entrance. "Take away the stone," he said. "But, Lord," said Martha, the sister of the dead man, "by this time there is a bad odor, for he has been there four days." Then Jesus said, "Did I not tell you that if you believe, you will see the glory of God?" So, they took away the stone. Then Jesus looked up and said, "Father, I thank you that you have heard me. I knew that you always hear me, but I said this for the benefit of the people standing here, that they may believe that you sent me." When he had said this, Jesus called in a loud voice, "Lazarus, come out!" The dead man came out, his hands and feet wrapped with strips of linen, and a cloth around his face. Jesus said to them, "Take off the grave clothes and let him go."

Discussion

In this verse Jesus prays to God in conversational form, and God answers Jesus with the miracle of reviving Lazarus.

Question: What do you think makes up a conversational prayer?

Answer: The three aspects of a conversational prayer are:

Talking to God like a friend

Asking God for guidance

Actively listening for an answer

The Lesson (30–40 min)

Activity/Practice

Return to the prayer posters. Have the students walk up and choose a sticky note to pray for. One sticky note per student. The teacher should give an example of how to conduct conversational prayer, then the students should go to their personal mats and privately pray for whatever is on their selected sticky note.

Example of conversational prayer:

Prayer request: I am very stressed today.

Conversational prayer: "Hey God, today has been really hard for this person. Do you think you could guide me in how I can help them today?"

Instruct students, once they've prayed over what's on the sticky note, to sit quietly and focus on listening for God to provide advice.

Some students won't come up with anything; others will be given the gift of response. Both situations are okay.

Once students feel their conversational prayer is complete, have them put the sticky notes on the "Prayed for" poster. If a solution was given, have the students put what God told them to do on a new sticky note and put that note on the "God said" poster.

If any student says they did not receive advice or guidance, reassure that this is okay. Sometimes God takes a while to respond. If possible, leave these boards up for the remaining weeks of class so students who heard nothing can update their response if needed.

Once everyone has completed the task, ask each person to share their experience.

Conversation

Conversational prayer is a form of spiritual self-care. Spending time talking to God and asking for advice and then actively listening for God to provide advice is one way we can work through our daily struggles. Throughout the next few weeks, we will go through various ways to experience spiritual self-care. Not every form of spiritual self-care will work for everyone. By learning and reviewing different ways to work through stress, anxiety, and depression, each student will be able to identify what works best for their personal faith and life journey.

Positive Affirmation (2–5 min)

This is the only part of the class that is not challenge by choice. Every student must participate.

Have the students go around the room and say one positive thing about themselves. This can be anything from something they like about their appearance to something they are good at. Follow this statement by "and I love myself." They key is specificity. The comment cannot be generic.

Example: "I have beautiful eyes, and I love myself."

Closing (5–10 min)

Have the students find a comfortable position to be in. This can be a laying down position. Tell the kids to breathe as deeply as they can in and then breathe as deeply as they can out. Have them do this two or three times with their eyes closed.

Meditation Script for the Week

Continue to breathe in (take a deep breath) *and out* (exhale).

As I count down from 5, I want you to picture your body sinking into the ground in the same way you sink into your bed.

5 . . . You relax your head and shoulders into your mat (take a deep breath in and out)

4 . . . You relax your neck and arms into your mat (take a deep breath in and out)

3 . . . You relax your hands and stomach, focusing on your breathing (take a deep breath in and out)

2 . . . You relax your legs and feet into your mat (take a deep breath in and out)

1 . . . You feel yourself drift into your safe space

In this space I want you to picture your perfect space. (Take a deep breath in and out)

This space is entirely your own. This can be a trail in the forest, a swimming hole in the ocean, a corner of your bedroom, in front of a fireplace on a camping trip, in a gaming community online, or any other place you can think of. (Take a deep breath in and out)

In this space, I want you to acknowledge the feeling this space gives you. Understand that you can be whoever God made you to be in this space. Safe. Secure. If your imagination wanders away from your safe space, focus back on your breathing, and when you are ready, head back into your space.

Trust Their Struggle

Now sit in this space for the next few minutes. Enjoy this time in your safe space. (Wait no less than two minutes in silence or with light music playing)

Now I am going to count you back home.

5 . . . You start to move away from your safe space and focus back on your breathing

4 . . . You start to wiggle your fingers, feeling the mat beneath you

3 . . . You start to wiggle your toes, focus on your breathing

2 . . . You bring awareness back to your whole self and open your eyes

1 . . . When you are ready, you can sit up

Then pray: "Lord, thank you for bringing us all together today in this space. We pray for each person in this room and their mental health. May you guide them to a place of peace, until we meet again."

Lesson 8: Devotional Meditation

Note to leader: this meeting should be no more than 1.5 hours. The point of this program is to educate but not to overwhelm.

Before the Meeting

If providing mats, place them on the floor with enough space between each one for each youth to reach their arms out without touching anyone else. If the youth are bringing their own mats, use brightly colored tape to denote spaces where their mats can be placed on the floor to ensure proper spacing.

Set up the gathering game by placing a piece of plain white printer paper on each mat, along with markers or crayons for each student. Set up the dry erase board in the front of the classroom so that every student can see the board.

Be sure to have the following items on hand:

Bible

Floor mats (if providing them)

Markers or Crayons

Plain white printer paper

Dry erase board/markers

Devotional Worksheet (provided in this packet)

Trust Their Struggle

Gathering (5–10 min)

Bible Story Pictionary

As the students arrive, ask them to take a seat on their mat and to draw their favorite Bible story on the plain paper in found on their mat. The students should keep their drawings private, and when complete, the teacher should collect each of the drawings.

Opening (10 min)

Teacher will hold up each picture, one at a time, and ask the students to guess which Bible story was drawn. The student who drew the picture should interact with this by informing their classmates if they are right or wrong. As the stories are guessed, the teacher should write on the dry erase board the title of the stories. For example, "The Great Flood" and "Jesus Rises from the Dead"

Opening Prayer (2 min)

"May we be blessed today by Your presence, Lord. May we understand more about Your Word and how we should conduct self-care. May You lift each of us up in You. Amen." (You can change the prayer to match your denomination or faith.)

The Lesson (30–40 min)

Group Devotions Activity

The teacher will go through each story listed on the dry erase board and ask students how this story might relate to their lives today. There are no wrong answers or interpretations, as this is individual. The purpose of this exercise is to encourage the students to look at the Bible in the context of their own lives.

The teacher explains devotional meditation:

> This activity everyone participated in is devotions as a group. Devotional meditation is when we do this same activity but on our own in personal communication with God. Sometimes when we take the time to actively listen to what God is trying to tell us we can find solutions and peace to what is currently triggering our difficult emotions.

Devotional Meditation Practical Application

For older students, hand out the daily devotion worksheet to each student. Ask them to read and reflect on how this devotional reading is relevant in their current situation. They can write or draw on the paper but must answer each block on the worksheet.

For younger students, hand out the daily devotion worksheet to each student, then read the devotional to the students, and then ask them to take a few moments to think about the devotional. Read each block to them and then let them answer each one at their own pace. Inform the students that if they have a question, they can raise their hand to minimize disruption.

Allow the students to sit in this space for five to ten minutes. Once complete if anyone would like to share their experience they can do so now.

Positive Affirmation (2–5 min)

This is the only part of the class that is not challenge by choice. Every student must participate.

Have the students go around the room and say one positive thing about themselves. This can be anything from something they like

about their appearance to something they are good at. Follow this statement by "and I love myself." They key is specificity. The comment cannot be generic.

Example: "I have beautiful eyes, and I love myself."

Closing (5–10 min)

Have the students find a comfortable position to be in. This can be a laying down position. Tell the kids to breathe as deeply as they can in, and then breathe as deeply as they can out. Have them do this two or three times with their eyes closed.

Meditation Script for the Week

Continue to breathe in (take a deep breath) *and out* (exhale).

As I count down from 5, I want you to picture your body sinking into the ground in the same way you sink into your bed.

5 . . . You relax your head and shoulders into your mat (take a deep breath in and out)

4 . . . You relax your neck and arms into your mat (take a deep breath in and out)

3 . . . You relax your hands and stomach, focusing on your breathing (take a deep breath in and out)

2 . . . You relax your legs and feet into your mat (take a deep breath in and out)

1 . . . You feel yourself drift into your safe space

In this space I want you to picture your perfect space. (Take a deep breath in and out)

This space is entirely your own. This can be a trail in the forest, a swimming hole in the ocean, a corner of your bedroom, in front of a fireplace on a camping trip, in a gaming community online, or any other place you can think of. (Take a deep breath in and out)

In this space, I want you to acknowledge the feeling this space gives you. Understand that you can be whoever God made you to be in this space. Safe. Secure. If your imagination wanders away from your safe space, focus back on your breathing and when you are ready, head back into your space.

Now sit in this space for the next few minutes. Enjoy this time in your safe space. (Wait no less than two minutes in silence or with light music playing)

Now I am going to count you back home.

5 . . . You start to move away from your safe space and focus back on your breathing

4 . . . You start to wiggle your fingers, feeling the mat beneath you

3 . . . You start to wiggle your toes, focus on your breathing

2 . . . You bring awareness back to your whole self and open your eyes

1 . . . When you are ready, you can sit up

Then pray: "Lord, thank you for bringing us all together today in this space. We pray for each person in this room and their mental health. May you guide them to a place of peace, until we meet again."

Trust Their Struggle

The Israelites were at war with people called the Philistines. One day a giant Philistine soldier named Goliath yelled, "Send me on man to fight me. If he wins, we will leave." The Israelite Soldiers were afraid of Goliath, so they would not fight him. One day a young boy named David was willing and said, "God will protect me."

Goliath laughed when he saw David, who was small and weak. "You cannot win," Goliath said. He raised his sword just as David hurled a stone from his slingshot. The stone hit Goliath between the eyes and killed him. The Philistines fled, and David became a hero.

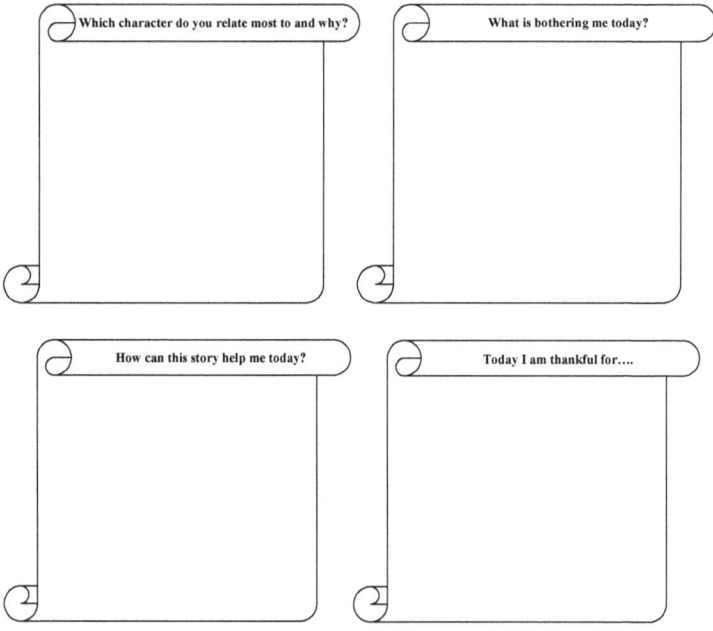

Lesson 9: Vigil Meditation

Note to leader: this meeting should be no more than 1.5 hours. The point of this program is to educate but not to overwhelm.

Before the Meeting

If providing mats, place them on the floor with enough space between each one for each youth to reach their arms out without touching anyone else. If the youth are bringing their own mats, use brightly colored tape to denote spaces where their mats can be placed on the floor to ensure proper spacing.

Set up the gathering activity. Place the box of vigil objects in the front of the room. Set up the teacher vigil on the front of the teachers mat as an example.

Provide a small box, a bag of sand (enough to fill the bottom), glue, popsicle sticks, and 4 fake flowers to each student.

Be sure to have the following items on hand:

Bible

Floor mats (if providing them)

Box of vigil objects

This box should include enough objects for each child to pick at least two items.

Item ideas:

Cross

Rosary

Trust Their Struggle

Candles (electric are best for kids)

If you have students of other faiths, provide objects related to their own faith.

Miniature Bibles

Pictures of religious figures or events

Other religious related objects

One small box per student

One bag of sand per student

Glue

Fake flowers

Five popsicle sticks per student.

One pinwheel per student

Gathering (10–15 min)

As students arrive, allow them to go to the box and select at least two items. Give the students a few minutes to set up their own vigil.

Instructions:

Dump the bag of sand into the bottom of the box and spread evenly.

Use the sticks, flowers, and two objects collected to build your own Zen Garden vigil.

Students can glue the popsicle sticks together to form an arch or create pathways in the sand.

Opening (10 min)

At this point all students should be sitting behind their own vigil. Ask if any student would like to share how they set up their vigil.

Practical Exercise Workbook

Once all students who chose to share have done so begin the opening prayer.

Opening Prayer (2 min)

"May we be blessed today by Your presence, Lord. May we understand more about Your Word and how we should conduct self-care. May You lift each of us up in You. Amen." (You can change the prayer to match your denomination or faith.)

Lesson

Bible Story: Matt 17:1-8

> Six days later, Jesus took Peter, James, and John, the brother of James, up on a high mountain by themselves. While they watched, Jesus' appearance was changed; his face became bright like the sun, and his clothes became white as light. Then Moses and Elijah appeared to them, talking with Jesus. Peter said to Jesus, "Lord, it is good that we are here. If you want, I will put up three tents here—one for you, one for Moses, and one for Elijah." While Peter was talking, a bright cloud covered them. A voice came from the cloud and said, "This is my Son, whom I love, and I am very pleased with him. Listen to him!" When his followers heard the voice, they were so frightened they fell to the ground. But Jesus went to them and touched them and said, "Stand up. Don't be afraid." When they looked up, they saw Jesus was now alone.

Discussion

In this verse Jesus is standing high up on a mountain praying for comfort from his Father. He knows he is about to be crucified, and in several instances in the Gospels, Jesus utilizes prayer meditation or vigil meditation in order to seek comfort and guidance. In essence, Jesus is practicing spiritual self-care in the way that best speaks to him. Moses and Elijah, who had transitioned into the next life long ago, greet Jesus on the mountain to provide the comfort he needs. The Scripture describes the lights as warm and welcoming.

In the same way, today we will discuss and practice vigil meditation. Things like lights, candles, and incense can help set the tone for proper meditation.

The Lesson (30–40 min)

For this lesson, we will be doing two types of vigil meditation.

Question: Can anyone tell me why we call this vigil meditation?

Answer: We pray and meditate in front of an interactive vigil that helps focus our energy and prayers.

NOTE: If students have trouble sitting still without any movement, providing the student with a fork to use as a rake in the sand during the meditation is a good way to maintain focus. Students can draw in the sand while the teacher is instructing the class.

Learning to Breathe

Hand each student a pinwheel. Have the students sit up straight and take in a deep breath, then blow the breath out with the intent of moving the pinwheel. Encourage students to see how long they can keep the pinwheel moving with one breath. Have the students practice these three or four times.

Learning about Mantras

Question: Can anyone tell me what a mantra is?

Answer: A word or phrase that helps an individual focus during meditation.

Question: What are some examples of a mantra?

Answer: Breathing in and out, Ohm, God's love, etc. (Allow students to come up with their own.)

Combining Breathing with Mantras

Have students take a deep breath in, whisper their mantra, then let the breath out. Have students practice this five times on their own.

Practical Application with Guided Meditation

Teacher reads the following:

Sitting with your legs crossed in front of your vigil, gently close your eyes and take in a nice, deep breath. Feel the cool air enter your nose and flow all the way down to your belly. Exhale slowly. Imagine breathing in peace and calm and exhaling out tension and stress. And again, paying close attention to your in-breath and your out-breath. Very good. Now you can just breathe comfortably and naturally. If you begin to lose focus, bring yourself back with the mantra you chose.

With your eyes closed, let's imagine the swirling energy centers in our body now, one by one as I lead you.

At the base of your spine is the first energy center. It is red in color. This center spins brightly when you feel safe and secure and when we release our fears. So, breathe in a soft red mist now, and breathe out any fears. Say aloud or to yourself, "I am safe. I am secure." Imagine this center spinning a warm, comforting red and flowing freely.

Your second energy center is orange and located right below your belly button. It spins brightly when you feel happy, friendly, and creative. It also likes when you release guilt and blame. So, breathe

Trust Their Struggle

in soft orange and let it fill your entire body. Focus right below your bellybutton and imagine the swirly bright orange color spinning around and around. Breathe in happiness, playfulness, and creativity. It feels so good.

Now we have the beautiful yellow energy center right above your tummy. This yellow energy shines brightly with strength, confidence, bravery, and motivation. Breathe all those things in on a warm yellow ray of sunshine. Let go of disappointments and focus on the warm yellow feeling.

In our heart area now, we have the green energy center of love. Release any sadness in your heart, and inhale the healing green mist, which carries love, kindness, forgiveness, and gratitude. These are the things that brighten up our heart center. Feel it shining so bright now as your heart area fills with all these wonderful things

Next, we have our beautiful blue energy center that rests in the throat area. It flows when we speak truth, when we are courageous, and when we speak up for ourselves and others. So, imagine breathing deeply in a beautiful blue brave mist. It travels to your throat area and grows bigger and bigger as you say to yourself, "I can express myself and say what I think and feel easily."

In the middle of your forehead is the indigo-colored energy center of mindfulness and intuition. Imagine breathing in the indigo colored-mist and watch as it creates a whirlwind of swirling color all around you now. This energy center shines brightly when we connect with and acknowledge our inner knowing, and when we see beyond appearances.

Finally, your crown energy center, like a beautiful violet flower opening at the top of your head, shines its radiant energy. We let go of attachments to free this energy to be its best. We let imagination, and the magic of knowing we are part of the whole cosmos, lead the way.

All of these centers are part of who we are even if we cannot see them with our eyes. You've done a great job today and remember to keep your centers clear with your rainbow breathing and focusing on the good things that each one represents.

(Script taken from https://www.greenchildmagazine.com/guided-chakra-meditation-for-beginners-and-kids-inner-rainbow/)

Mantra Meditation

Students work toward expressing a group mantra.

Students breath in deeply, then on the exhale say "aaaaaaaaah" to the breath's conclusion.

Students breath in deeply, then on the exhale say "oooooooooh" to the breath's conclusion.

Students breath in deeply, then on the exhale say "mmmmmmm" to the breath's conclusion.

Have students repeat this cycle three times. Eyes can be closed or open. They are learning to focus their mantra through mantra meditation.

Discussion

Question: How can these practices be applied when we are stressed or anxious?

Answer: Learning to breath before, during, and after a trigger can help us to learn to control our anxiety and our reaction to our triggering events.

Positive Affirmation (2–5 min)

This is the only part of the class that is not challenge by choice. Every student must participate.

Have the students go around the room and say one positive thing about themselves. This can be anything from something they like

Trust Their Struggle

about their appearance to something they are good at. Follow this statement by "and I love myself." They key is specificity. The comment cannot be generic.

Example: "I have beautiful eyes, and I love myself."

Closing (5–10 min)

"Lord, thank you for bringing us all together today in this space. We pray for each person in this room and their mental health. May you guide them to a place of peace, until we meet again."

Lesson 10: Forest Bathing

Note to leader: this meeting should be no more than 1.5 hours. The point of this program is to educate but not to overwhelm.

Before the Meeting

This class should be done outside on a hiking trail.

Be sure to have the following items on hand:

Small bottle of lavender essential oil

Extra bottles of water for students

First-aid kit

Cotton balls

Gathering (5–10 min)

As students arrive, have them stand in a circle.

Opening (10 min)

Discussion

Question: Can anyone tell me what a forest bath is and where it came from?

Answer: Forest bathing was created in 1980 in Japan as a way to combat anxiety and stress after a long work week. Forest bathing is when you take an essential oil linked to relaxation, like lavender, breath it in, share a devotional, and then walk in silence on a set trail through a forest.

Opening Prayer (2 min)

"May we be blessed today by Your presence, Lord. May we understand more about Your Word and how we should conduct self-care. May You lift each of us up in You. Amen." (You can change the prayer to match your denomination or faith.)

The Lesson (30–40 min)

Essential Oil Inhalation

Give each student a cotton ball and place a single drop of essential oil on it. Students should then bring the cotton ball to their nose and inhale the lavender scent. Have the students take in two or three deep breaths before continuing.

Question: Can anyone tell me why we inhale lavender before the hike?

Answer: Lavender has been linked to relaxation and stress relief which can help with stress and anxiety.

Devotional

The teacher should read the following devotional prior to stepping off on the hike.

Rev 22:1–2:

> And he showed me a river of the water of life, clear as crystal, coming from the throne of God and of the Lamb, in the middle of its street. On either side of the river was the tree of life, bearing twelve kinds of fruit, yielding its

fruit every month; and the leaves of the tree were for the healing of the nations.

Say: "God calls us to be stewards of the earth and provides us with a sense of peace when we engage with his creation. As you hike through the forest, think about how this verse applies to your life."

Instructions

Students should walk in a straight line down the path with the teacher in the lead.

This is a silent hike. Students should focus on their breathing and the mantra of their choice as they walk. Encourage them to silently take in their surroundings.

At roughly the halfway point of the chosen hike, stop and have the students sit in a circle.

Grounding

Discussion

Question: Does anyone know what grounding is?

Answer: Grounding is a technique used to center ourselves back into balance when we feel overly stressed or anxious.

Practical Application

Ask the students to take off their socks and shoes and stand with their feet shoulder-width apart. Ask the students to lift their arms and hands above their heads and stand as tall as they can without lifting any part of their feet off the ground. The students should now close their eyes and imagine that their feet are growing roots. These roots anchor them to the ground and spread across the forest floor. Tell the students to imagine that they are growing tall very quickly and will soon be taller than the tallest trees in the forest. We are grounding ourselves into our surroundings.

When they are ready, the students can open their eyes, bring their hands down to their side, and take a seat.

Tell the students they can put their shoes back on.

Completing the Forest Bath

The group should finish the hike in silence, walking in a straight line.

Once the forest bath hike is complete, have the students stand or sit in a circle and continue to positive affirmations for the day.

Positive Affirmation (2–5 min)

This is the only part of the class that is not challenge by choice. Every student must participate.

Have the students go around the room and say one positive thing about themselves. This can be anything from something they like about their appearance to something they are good at. Follow this statement by "and I love myself." They key is specificity. The comment cannot be generic.

Example: "I have beautiful eyes, and I love myself."

Closing (5–10 min)

"Lord, thank you for bringing us all together today in this space. We pray for each person in this room and their mental health. May you guide them to a place of peace, until we meet again."

Lesson 11: Creative Spirituality (Art)

Note to leader: this meeting should be no more than 1.5 hours. The point of this program is to educate but not to overwhelm.

Before the Meeting

If providing mats, place them on the floor with enough space between each one for each youth to reach their arms out without touching anyone else. If the youth are bringing their own mats, use brightly colored tape to denote spaces where their mats can be placed on the floor to ensure proper spacing.

Set up the gathering activity.

Provide each student with a small canvas board and a packet of markers on their mat.

Be sure to have the following items on hand:

Bible

Floor mats (if providing them)

One canvas per student

One pack of markers per student

Gathering (5–10 min)

As students arrive ask them to trace one of their hands on the canvas. Once complete, have them put their markers down. Assist the younger students as needed with tracing.

Opening (10 min)

Question: Can anyone tell me why art is a form of spiritual self-care?

Answer: Art helps us refocus our energy on something beautiful. It can help us to commune with God and often sends us into a state of relaxation when we are stressed out.

Opening Prayer: (2 min)

"May we be blessed today by Your presence, Lord. May we understand more about Your Word and how we should conduct self-care. May You lift each of us up in You. Amen." (You can change the prayer to match your denomination or faith.)

Lesson

Bible Story

Gen 1:1–26

> In the beginning God created the heavens and the earth. Now the earth was formless and empty, darkness was over the surface of the deep, and the Spirit of God was hovering over the waters. And God said, "Let there be light," and there was light. God saw that the light was good, and he separated the light from the darkness. God called the light "day," and the darkness he called "night." And there was evening, and there was morning—the first day.
>
> And God said, "Let there be a vault between the waters to separate water from water." So God made the vault and separated the water under the vault from the water above it. And it was so. God called the vault "sky." And there was evening, and there was morning—the second day.
>
> And God said, "Let the water under the sky be gathered to one place, and let dry ground appear." And it was

so. God called the dry ground "land," and the gathered waters he called "seas." And God saw that it was good.

Then God said, "Let the land produce vegetation: seed-bearing plants and trees on the land that bear fruit with seed in it, according to their various kinds." And it was so. The land produced vegetation: plants bearing seed according to their kinds and trees bearing fruit with seed in it according to their kinds. And God saw that it was good. And there was evening, and there was morning—the third day.

And God said, "Let there be lights in the vault of the sky to separate the day from the night and let them serve as signs to mark sacred times, and days and years, and let them be lights in the vault of the sky to give light on the earth." And it was so. God made two great lights—the greater light to govern the day and the lesser light to govern the night. He also made the stars. God set them in the vault of the sky to give light on the earth, to govern the day and the night, and to separate light from darkness. And God saw that it was good. And there was evening, and there was morning—the fourth day.

And God said, "Let the water teem with living creatures, and let birds fly above the earth across the vault of the sky." So, God created the great creatures of the sea and every living thing with which the water teems and that moves about in it, according to their kinds, and every winged bird according to its kind. And God saw that it was good. God blessed them and said, "Be fruitful and increase in number and fill the water in the seas, and let the birds increase on the earth." And there was evening, and there was morning—the fifth day.

And God said, "Let the land produce living creatures according to their kinds: the livestock, the creatures that move along the ground, and the wild animals, each according to its kind." And it was so. God made the wild animals according to their kinds, the livestock according to their kinds, and all the creatures that move along the ground according to their kinds. And God saw that it was good.

Then God said, "Let us make mankind in our image, in our likeness, so that they may rule over the fish in the sea and the birds in the sky, over the livestock and all the wild animals, and over all the creatures that move along the ground."

Discussion

Question: Why do you think this verse is relevant to artistic spiritual self-care?

Answer: God highly valued the gift of creation. He himself created the heavens and the earth and everything in it. They were like clay molds that he breathed life into.

Say: As we work through today's lesson, keep this story in mind.

The Lesson (30–40 min)

Hand of Positive Affirmation Activity

Say: "There are many ways to experience spiritual self-care through art. For today's lesson we are going to draw on our canvas different positive aspects of ourselves. You can draw on or around your hand outline pictures of activities you love or your favorite things about yourself. Your project should have a minimum of five positive affirmations. We will work in silence. If you have trouble thinking of something to draw or write, take a moment, close your eyes, take in a deep breath, and ask God to guide your thoughts."

Give the students twenty minutes to complete this task.

Sharing

Ask if any of the students would like to share their hand. Once everyone has shared, complete the weekly positive affirmation exercise.

Positive Affirmation (2–5 min)

This is the only part of the class that is not challenge by choice. Every student must participate. Have the students go around the room and say one positive thing about themselves. This can be anything from something they like about their appearance to something they are good at. Follow this statement by "and I love myself." They key is specificity. The comment cannot be generic.

Example: "I have beautiful eyes, and I love myself."

Discussion

Question: Why is it important to say kind things to ourselves?

Answer: Understanding what our value is and acknowledging our strengths out loud reminds us that we are valued and loved. Manifesting our gifts that God gave us through acknowledgment glorifies God and can help in deterring stress, anxiety, and even suicidal ideation.

Closing (5–10 min)

Have the students find a comfortable position to be in. This can be a laying down position. Tell the kids to breath as deeply as they can in, and then breath as deeply as they can out. Have them do this two or three times with their eyes closed.

Meditation Script for the Week

Now, just breathe normally and relax.

Imagine you are floating through the air.

Feel the wind in your hair, gently billowing on the breeze.

You can hear birds flying around you, and the smell of fresh rain fills the air.

Practical Exercise Workbook

Imagine you gently land on a rainbow.

The color red glows brighter then the rest and slowly envelops you into a warm hug.

As you breathe in the color red you feel a sense of security. Think to yourself, "I am safe."

As the color red fades, the color orange begins to glow brighter than the rest and slowly envelops you into a warm hug.

As you breathe in the color orange, you feel a sense of control. Think to yourself, "I have self-control."

As the color orange fades, the color yellow begins to glow brighter than the rest and slowly envelops you into a warm hug.

As you breathe in the color yellow, you feel a sense of happiness. Think to yourself, "I am happy."

As the color yellow fades, the color green begins to glow brighter than the rest and slowly envelops you into a warm hug.

As you breathe in the color green, you feel a sense of growth. Think to yourself, "I am healthy."

As the color green fades, the color blue begins to glow brighter than the rest and slowly envelops you into a warm hug.

As you breathe in the color blue, you feel a sense of calm. Think to yourself, "I am at peace.

As the color blue fades, the color indigo begins to glow brighter than the rest and slowly envelops you into a warm hug.

As you breathe in the color indigo, you feel a sense of wisdom. Think to yourself, "I am smart."

As the color indigo fades, the color violet begins to glow brighter than the rest and slowly envelops you into a warm hug.

As you breathe in the color violet, you feel a sense of creativity. Think to yourself, "I am creative."

As the color indigo fades, picture yourself floating away from the rainbow. As you move away from the rainbow, you notice the entire

Trust Their Struggle

rainbow is glowing bright. Think to yourself, "I am exactly who I was created to be, and I love myself for who I am and who I will become."

As you float back down to earth, begin to feel the ground beneath you.

Take a deep breath in, and wiggle your fingers and toes.

Take another deep breath, and when you are ready, open your eyes.[1]

Then pray: "Lord, thank you for bringing us all together today in this space. We pray for each person in this room and their mental health. May you guide them to a place of peace, until we meet again."

---

1. Slander, "Rainbow Meditation Script."

Lesson 12: Creative Spirituality (Movement)

Note to leader: this meeting should be no more than 1.5 hours. The point of this program is to educate but not to overwhelm.

Before the Meeting

If providing mats, place them on the floor with enough space between each one for each youth to reach their arms out without touching anyone else. If the youth are bringing their own mats, use brightly colored tape to denote spaces where their mats can be placed on the floor to ensure proper spacing.

Be sure to have the following items on hand:

Bible

Floor mats (if providing them)

Ribbon sticks

Bluetooth speaker (or another device to play controlled music on)

Gathering (5–10 min)

As the students arrive have them find their mat and take a seat.

Opening (10 min)

Once everyone is seated, begin with the opening prayer.

Opening Prayer (2 min)

"May we be blessed today by Your presence, Lord. May we understand more about Your Word and how we should conduct self-care. May You lift each of us up in You. Amen." (You can change the prayer to match your denomination or faith.)

Lesson

Bible Story

Ps 30:11–12

> You turned my wailing into dancing; you removed my sackcloth and clothed me with joy, that my heart may sing your praises and not be silent. LORD my God, I will praise you forever.

Discussion

Question: Do you think dancing can be a form of spiritual self-care? (Allow students to respond. There is no wrong answer.)

Say: "Last week we learned that God valued creativity and practiced it himself. Dance has long been linked to spirituality and self-care in cultures across the world. In the same way, we can glorify and move closer to God through dance."

The Lesson (30–40 min)

Ribbon Dance Activity

Hand out the ribbon sticks to each of the students.

Say: "When I start the music, dance around the room. Be mindful of others around you while remembering to listen for Gods voice as you move. Try to dance to the rhythm of the music that I play."

At this point the teacher can turn on any music they feel is appropriate. If working with students outside the Christian faith, ask for suggestions from their culture. Be open to suggestions given.

As the music plays, the students should move around the room with their ribbon, dancing in silence however the spirit inspires them. Allow this to continue for the length of two or three songs.

Discussion

At the conclusion of the final song, ask the students to return to hand you back their ribbon stick and take a seat back onto their mat.

Question: Did anyone experience the spirit move through them?

If students say yes, encourage them to explain how they felt in those moments.

Say: When we dance with the purpose of allowing the spirit to guide us, we can find ourselves in a trance like state. In these moments we can talk to God about how our day went and where we need his help, and actively listen for advice or guidance.

Positive Affirmation (2–5 min)

This is the only part of the class that is not challenge by choice. Every student must participate.

Have the students go around the room and say one positive thing about themselves. This can be anything from something they like about their appearance to something they are good at. Follow this statement by "and I love myself." They key is specificity. The comment cannot be generic.

Example: "I have beautiful eyes, and I love myself."

Closing (5–10 min)

Have the students find a comfortable position to be in. This can be a laying down position. Tell the kids to breath as deeply as they can in, and then breath as deeply as they can out. Have them do this two or three times with their eyes closed.

Meditation Script for the Week

Now, just breathe normally and relax.

Imagine you are floating through the air.

Feel the wind in your hair, gently billowing on the breeze.

You can hear birds flying around you, and the smell of fresh rain fills the air.

Imagine you gently land on a rainbow.

The color red glows brighter then the rest and slowly envelops you into a warm hug.

As you breathe in the color red you feel a sense of security. Think to yourself, "I am safe."

As the color red fades, the color orange begins to glow brighter than the rest and slowly envelops you into a warm hug.

As you breathe in the color orange, you feel a sense of control. Think to yourself, "I have self-control."

As the color orange fades, the color yellow begins to glow brighter than the rest and slowly envelops you into a warm hug.

As you breathe in the color yellow, you feel a sense of happiness. Think to yourself, "I am happy."

As the color yellow fades, the color green begins to glow brighter than the rest and slowly envelops you into a warm hug.

As you breathe in the color green, you feel a sense of growth. Think to yourself, "I am healthy."

As the color green fades, the color blue begins to glow brighter than the rest and slowly envelops you into a warm hug.

As you breathe in the color blue, you feel a sense of calm. Think to yourself, "I am at peace."

As the color blue fades, the color indigo begins to glow brighter than the rest and slowly envelops you into a warm hug.

As you breathe in the color indigo, you feel a sense of wisdom. Think to yourself, "I am smart."

As the color indigo fades, the color violet begins to glow brighter than the rest and slowly envelops you into a warm hug.

As you breathe in the color violet, you feel a sense of creativity. Think to yourself, "I am creative."

As the color indigo fades, picture yourself floating away from the rainbow. As you move away from the rainbow, you notice the entire rainbow is glowing bright. Think to yourself, "I am exactly who I was created to be, and I love myself for who I am and who I will become."

As you float back down to earth, begin to feel the ground beneath you.

Take a deep breath in, and wiggle your fingers and toes.

Take another deep breath, and when you are ready, open your eyes.

Then pray: "Lord, thank you for bringing us all together today in this space. We pray for each person in this room and their mental health. May you guide them to a place of peace, until we meet again."

Lesson 13: Creative Spirituality (Written)

Note to leader: this meeting should be no more than 1.5 hours. The point of this program is to educate but not to overwhelm.

Before the Meeting

If providing mats, keep them rolled up with you. As students arrive, hand them out.

This lesson is best done in an outdoor setting.

Be sure to have the following items on hand:

Bible

Floor mats (if providing them)

Three attached worksheets per student

Markers/crayons/colored pencils

Lap desks for outdoor use

Gathering (5–10 min)

As the students arrive, have them collect a floor mat and find a quiet spot in the outdoor space. Ensure students are separated from one another by several feet.

Opening (10 min)

Begin today's lesson with the opening prayer.

Opening Prayer (2 min)

"May we be blessed today by Your presence, Lord. May we understand more about Your Word and how we should conduct self-care. May You lift each of us up in You. Amen." (You can change the prayer to match your denomination or faith.)

Lesson Bible Story

Jer 30:1-3

> The word that came to Jeremiah from the Lord, saying, "This is what the Lord, the God of Israel says: 'Write all the words which I have spoken to you in a book. For behold, days are coming,' declares the Lord, 'when I will restore the fortunes of My people Israel and Judah.' The Lord says, 'I will also bring them back to the land that I gave to their forefathers, and they shall take possession of it.'"

Discussion

Question: Why do you think it might be helpful to write down the things we hear God tell us while meditating?

Answer: God encourages us to write these things down so we remember his advice and return to it as needed.

Question: What other things can be written about while meditating?

Answer: We can write down our frustrations in a letter to God. This helps us to express how we are feeling and allows an outlet for our emotions.

The Lesson (30–40 min)

Say: Today we are going to practice spiritual self-care through journaling or writing. We will go through the process three times with three different prompts.

For the first prompt the students will sit in silence and practice their purposeful breathing with their eyes closed for three to five breaths. As the student is breathing they should be listening to their surroundings. After they complete the breathing exercise, have the students journal about what they observed around them. The worksheet has a spot to draw and write about their observations. Students can journal through drawing, through writing, or through both.

For the second prompt students will write or draw about anything that is currently bothering them. Use this time as an outlet for any anger, stress, or anxiety they might be feeling.

For the third prompt students should sit in silence for a moment and listen for God. Encourage the students to think about any blessings they have in their life. They should write or draw anything positive that comes to mind on this final sheet.

When the students have completed all three prompts, they can be encouraged to share their experiences.

Positive Affirmation (2–5 min)

This is the only part of the class that is not challenge by choice. Every student must participate.

Have the students go around the room and say one positive thing about themselves. This can be anything from something they like

about their appearance to something they are good at. Follow this statement by "and I love myself." They key is specificity. The comment cannot be generic.

Example: "I have beautiful eyes, and I love myself."

Closing (5-10 min)

Now, just breathe normally and relax.

Imagine you are floating through the air.

Feel the wind in your hair, gently billowing on the breeze.

You can hear birds flying around you, and the smell of fresh rain fills the air.

Imagine you gently land on a rainbow.

The color red glows brighter then the rest and slowly envelops you into a warm hug.

As you breathe in the color red you feel a sense of security. Think to yourself, "I am safe."

As the color red fades, the color orange begins to glow brighter than the rest and slowly envelops you into a warm hug.

As you breathe in the color orange, you feel a sense of control. Think to yourself, "I have self-control."

As the color orange fades, the color yellow begins to glow brighter than the rest and slowly envelops you into a warm hug.

As you breathe in the color yellow, you feel a sense of happiness. Think to yourself, "I am happy."

As the color yellow fades, the color green begins to glow brighter than the rest and slowly envelops you into a warm hug.

As you breathe in the color green, you feel a sense of growth. Think to yourself, "I am healthy."

As the color green fades, the color blue begins to glow brighter than the rest and slowly envelops you into a warm hug.

Trust Their Struggle

As you breathe in the color blue, you feel a sense of calm. Think to yourself, "I am at peace."

As the color blue fades, the color indigo begins to glow brighter than the rest and slowly envelops you into a warm hug.

As you breathe in the color indigo, you feel a sense of wisdom. Think to yourself, "I am smart."

As the color indigo fades, the color violet begins to glow brighter than the rest and slowly envelops you into a warm hug.

As you breathe in the color violet, you feel a sense of creativity. Think to yourself, "I am creative."

As the color indigo fades, picture yourself floating away from the rainbow. As you move away from the rainbow, you notice the entire rainbow is glowing bright. Think to yourself, "I am exactly who I was created to be, and I love myself for who I am and who I will become."

As you float back down to earth, begin to feel the ground beneath you.

Take a deep breath in, and wiggle your fingers and toes.

Take another deep breath, and when you are ready, open your eyes.

Then pray: "Lord, thank you for bringing us all together today in this space. We pray for each person in this room and their mental health. May you guide them to a place of peace until we meet again."

Practical Exercise Workbook

Lesson 14: Christian Yoga Meditation

Note to leader: this meeting should be no more than 1.5 hours. The point of this program is to educate but not to overwhelm.

Before the Meeting

If providing mats, place them on the floor with enough space between each one for each youth to reach their arms out without touching anyone else. If the youth are bringing their own mats, use brightly colored tape to denote spaces where their mats can be placed on the floor to ensure proper spacing.

Be sure to have the following items on hand:

Bible

Floor mats (if providing them)

Meditation music

One routine worksheet per student

Gathering (5–10 min)

As students arrive have them collect a routine worksheet and find their mat.

Opening (10 min)

Begin today's lesson with the opening prayer.

Opening Prayer (2 min)

"May we be blessed today by Your presence, Lord. May we understand more about Your Word and how we should conduct self-care. May You lift each of us up in You. Amen." (You can change the prayer to match your denomination or faith.)

Lesson Bible Story

Ps 46:10

> He says, "Be still, and know that I am God; I will be exalted among the nations, I will be exalted in the earth."

Discussion

Question: Today we are doing to learn about Christian yoga. What does this verse tell us to do that might apply to yoga?

Answer: God tells us to "be still." Being still is not a common practice for us. Yoga is a practice that takes small movements to stretch and center ourselves so we can connect with the divine.

The Lesson (30–40 min)

Say: "We will go through the yoga routine once together. Then I will hand out a worksheet with the routine, so you can use it as a reference if you would like. You will spend a few minutes moving through the yoga routine on your own, at your own pace. When moving through the routine on your own you do not need to follow the routine, you can add your own movements or stretches. The routine is a guide, not a rule."

The teacher should turn on the meditation music. Have the students start in the seated position on their mat and begin with completing three deep breath exercises before beginning the first routine.

Once the activity is complete, have the students complete the routine by conducting three deep breath exercises.

Positive Affirmation (2–5 min)

This is the only part of the class that is not challenge by choice. Every student must participate.

Have the students go around the room and say one positive thing about themselves. This can be anything from something they like about their appearance to something they are good at. Follow this statement by "and I love myself." They key is specificity. The comment cannot be generic.

Example: "I have beautiful eyes, and I love myself."

Closing (5–10 min)

Now, just breathe normally and relax.

Imagine you are floating through the air.

Feel the wind in your hair, gently billowing on the breeze.

You can hear birds flying around you, and the smell of fresh rain fills the air.

Imagine you gently land on a rainbow.

The color red glows brighter then the rest and slowly envelops you into a warm hug.

As you breathe in the color red you feel a sense of security. Think to yourself, "I am safe."

As the color red fades, the color orange begins to glow brighter than the rest and slowly envelops you into a warm hug.

As you breathe in the color orange, you feel a sense of control. Think to yourself, "I have self-control."

As the color orange fades, the color yellow begins to glow brighter than the rest and slowly envelops you into a warm hug.

As you breathe in the color yellow, you feel a sense of happiness. Think to yourself, "I am happy."

As the color yellow fades, the color green begins to glow brighter than the rest and slowly envelops you into a warm hug.

As you breathe in the color green, you feel a sense of growth. Think to yourself, "I am healthy."

As the color green fades, the color blue begins to glow brighter than the rest and slowly envelops you into a warm hug.

As you breathe in the color blue, you feel a sense of calm. Think to yourself, "I am at peace.

As the color blue fades, the color indigo begins to glow brighter than the rest and slowly envelops you into a warm hug.

As you breathe in the color indigo, you feel a sense of wisdom. Think to yourself, "I am smart."

As the color indigo fades, the color violet begins to glow brighter than the rest and slowly envelops you into a warm hug.

As you breathe in the color violet, you feel a sense of creativity. Think to yourself, "I am creative."

As the color indigo fades, picture yourself floating away from the rainbow. As you move away from the rainbow, you notice the entire rainbow is glowing bright. Think to yourself, "I am exactly who I was created to be, and I love myself for who I am and who I will become."

As you float back down to earth, begin to feel the ground beneath you.

Take a deep breath in, and wiggle your fingers and toes.

Take another deep breath, and when you are ready, open your eyes.

Trust Their Struggle

Then pray: "Lord, thank you for bringing us all together today in this space. We pray for each person in this room and their mental health. May you guide them to a place of peace, until we meet again."

Lesson 15: Active Listening Meditation

Note to leader: this meeting should be no more than 1.5 hours. The point of this program is to educate but not to overwhelm.

Before the Meeting

If providing mats, place them on the floor with enough space between each one for each youth to reach their arms out without touching anyone else. If the youth are bringing their own mats, use brightly colored tape to denote spaces where their mats can be placed on the floor to ensure proper spacing.

Be sure to have the following items on hand:

Bible

Floor mats (if providing them)

Singing bowl

One worksheet per student

Gathering (5–10 min)

As students arrive, have students go find their seat.

Opening (10 min)

Begin today's lesson with the opening prayer.

Opening Prayer (2 min)

"May we be blessed today by Your presence, Lord. May we understand more about Your Word and how we should conduct self-care. May You lift each of us up in You. Amen." (You can change the prayer to match your denomination or faith.)

Lesson Bible Story

Prov 19:20-21

> Listen to advice and accept instruction, that you may gain wisdom in the future. Many are the plans in the mind of a man, but it is the purpose of the Lord that will stand.

Discussion

Question: What does this verse tell us about what God wants us to do when we listen?

Answer: God wants us to listen to what he has to say and follow his instructions.

Question: Do you think you will hear God speaking if you are not active listening?

Answer: No, God's voice can only be heard among the silence. We need to learn to actively listen in order to understand what God wants from us.

The Lesson (30-40 min)

Singing Bowl Exercise

Say: "We are going to do a couple of listening exercises to practice active listening. This is a singing bowl. This is used in many cultures. They originated in Tibet but are believed to be from a religion and group that predates Tibet and Buddhism. I want everyone to close their eyes. I am going to play the singing bowl at different sound levels. When you can no longer hear the bowl singing, open your eyes."

Begin exercise. Instructor can do this exercise more than once.

Discussion

Question: Was it easy or hard to be quiet and listen to one sound?

Question: Did you find that you got distracted while listening to the bell?

Question: What other sounds could you hear besides the bell?

Question: How did it feel in your body to be still and listen to sounds?

"What's That Sound?" Exercise

For this exercise, students choose their favorite animal to imitate. One at a time, students make the noise of their favorite animal and the other students have to guess what animal they are imitating.

Once every student has had a chance to act out their sound, hand out the worksheet for the next exercise.

"What's That Sound?" Worksheet

Instructor should have students close their eyes, take three purposeful breaths, and then begin drawing or writing what they can hear on their worksheets.

Once everyone is done, students can share what they heard.

Positive Affirmation (2–5 min)

This is the only part of the class that is not challenge by choice. Every student must participate.

Have the students go around the room and say one positive thing about themselves. This can be anything from something they like about their appearance to something they are good at. Follow this statement by "and I love myself." They key is specificity. The comment cannot be generic.

Example: "I have beautiful eyes, and I love myself."

Closing (5–10 min)

Now, just breathe normally and relax.

Imagine you are floating through the air.

Feel the wind in your hair, gently billowing on the breeze.

You can hear birds flying around you, and the smell of fresh rain fills the air.

Imagine you gently land on a rainbow.

The color red glows brighter then the rest and slowly envelops you into a warm hug.

As you breathe in the color red you feel a sense of security. Think to yourself, "I am safe."

As the color red fades, the color orange begins to glow brighter than the rest and slowly envelops you into a warm hug.

As you breathe in the color orange, you feel a sense of control. Think to yourself, "I have self-control."

As the color orange fades, the color yellow begins to glow brighter than the rest and slowly envelops you into a warm hug.

As you breathe in the color yellow, you feel a sense of happiness. Think to yourself, "I am happy."

Practical Exercise Workbook

As the color yellow fades, the color green begins to glow brighter than the rest and slowly envelops you into a warm hug.

As you breathe in the color green, you feel a sense of growth. Think to yourself, "I am healthy."

As the color green fades, the color blue begins to glow brighter than the rest and slowly envelops you into a warm hug.

As you breathe in the color blue, you feel a sense of calm. Think to yourself, "I am at peace.

As the color blue fades, the color indigo begins to glow brighter than the rest and slowly envelops you into a warm hug.

As you breathe in the color indigo, you feel a sense of wisdom. Think to yourself, "I am smart."

As the color indigo fades, the color violet begins to glow brighter than the rest and slowly envelops you into a warm hug.

As you breathe in the color violet, you feel a sense of creativity. Think to yourself, "I am creative."

As the color indigo fades, picture yourself floating away from the rainbow. As you move away from the rainbow, you notice the entire rainbow is glowing bright. Think to yourself, "I am exactly who I was created to be, and I love myself for who I am and who I will become."

As you float back down to earth, begin to feel the ground beneath you.

Take a deep breath in, and wiggle your fingers and toes.

Take another deep breath, and when you are ready, open your eyes.

Then pray: "Lord, thank you for bringing us all together today in this space. We pray for each person in this room and their mental health. May you guide them to a place of peace until we meet again."

What sounds can I hear?

Lesson 16: Mantras Practice

Note to leader: this meeting should be no more than 1.5 hours. The point of this program is to educate but not to overwhelm.

Before the Meeting

If providing mats, place them on the floor with enough space between each one for each youth to reach their arms out without touching anyone else. If the youth are bringing their own mats, use brightly colored tape to denote spaces where their mats can be placed on the floor to ensure proper spacing.

Set up the gathering game. Hang five poster boards around the room. One symbol should be written on each board. See attached hand out for reference.

Be sure to have the following on hand:

Bible

Floor mats (if providing them)

Poster boards with reiki symbols

One handout per student

One stuffed animal per student

Gathering (5–10 min)

As the students arrive have them walk around the room and practice tracing the reiki symbols in the air with their finger. When they have completed each symbol, ask students to choose a stuffed animal on their way back to their mats.

Opening (10 min)

Begin with opening prayer.

Opening Prayer (2 min)

"May we be blessed today by Your presence, Lord. May we understand more about Your Word and how we should conduct self-care. May You lift each of us up in You. Amen." (You can change the prayer to match your denomination or faith.)

Lesson Bible Story

Luke 4:40

> Now when the sun was setting, all those who had any who were sick with various diseases brought them to him, and he laid his hands on every one of them and healed them.

Question: How does this verse support the use of reiki as Christians?

Answer: In many ways, when Jesus laid his hands upon a servant and healed that person, it was through the Holy Spirit. In the same way, we can utilize the gifts of the Holy Spirit to heal ourselves.

The Lesson (30–40 min)

Say: Today we are going to learn the practice of reiki on self. This is a pre-level one course.

The Chakras and Reiki Hand Positions

Go over each of the chakras and their meanings with the students. Read down the worksheet. Then ask students to identify which chakras they should focus on for various ailments in self-care.

Anxiety—Heart

Depression—Crown and Heart

Stress—Crown, Heart, and Sacral

Grounding—Root

Go over each of the colors of the chakras and their healing benefits. Explain that when meditating in reiki, the students should picture the color of the chakra they want to focus on. This information is also on their worksheets.

Reiki Principles

Reiki principles can be used as mantras while meditating. These principles are based on the idea that setting short, attainable goals for ourselves helps to build confidence and reduces stress. These mantras are "just for today" and are focused on a positive growth mindset. Have the students recite the following mantras:

Just for today, I release angry thoughts.

Just for today, I release thoughts of worry.

Just for today, I'm grateful.

Just for today, I expand my consciousness.

Just for today, I'm gentle with all beings.

Reiki Meditation: Bringing It All Together

Complete the following steps twice as a group. Then allow the students five to ten minutes to practice this on their own and ask for assistance as needed.

Trust Their Struggle

Step 1: Sit straight up on your mat. Eyes closed is ideal.

Step 2: Have the students place one hand on their head and one hand over their heart. We will focus on spirituality and self-love today.

Step 3: Students should then close their eyes and begin reciting their chosen mantra to themselves.

Step 4: Students should picture the color of the chakra they are focusing on.

Step 5: Allow students to meditate on this place, visualizing the pain or discomfort leaving their body.

Note: If students would prefer to state their mantra internally this is okay.

Positive Affirmation (2–5 min)

This is the only part of the class that is not challenge by choice. Every student must participate.

Have the students go around the room and say one positive thing about themselves. This can be anything from something they like about their appearance to something they are good at. Follow this statement by "and I love myself". They key is specificity. The comment cannot be generic.

Example: "I have beautiful eyes, and I love myself".

Closing (5–10 min)

Then pray: "Lord, thank you for bringing us all together today in this space. We pray for each person in this room and their mental health. May you guide them to a place of peace until we meet again."

Practical Exercise Workbook

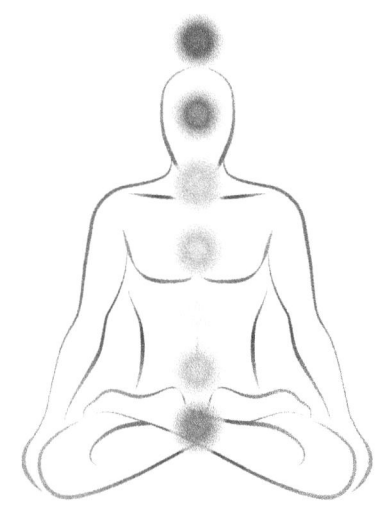

Crown Chakra

Third Eye Chakra

Throat Chakra

Heart Chakra

Solar Plexus Chakra

Sacral Chakra

Root Chakra

Crown	Spirituality
Third Eye	Self-Awareness
Throat	Communication
Heart	Self-Love
Solar Plexus	Wisdom
Sacral	Creativity
Root	Grounding

Reiki Principles and Mantras

- Just for today, I release angry thoughts
- Just for today, I release thoughts of worry
- Just for today, I'm grateful
- Just for today, I expand my consciousness
- Just for today, I'm gentle with all beings

Lesson 17: Developing the Spiritual Care Plan

Note to leader: this meeting should be no more than 1.5 hours. The point of this program is to educate but not to overwhelm.

Before the Meeting

If providing mats, keep the mats rolled up in a single spot for collection by the student during the gathering.

Set up the gathering activity. Set aside ten different spots around the room dedicated to the ten different types of spiritual self-care covered in this course. Each section should have all the materials needed for the student to properly conduct their chosen form of self-care.

Be sure to have the following items on hand:

Bible

Floor mats (if providing them)

Extra worksheets from each lesson

Poster board for labeling each dedicated space

Conversational prayer

Open space to lay out mats

Devotional meditation

Devotional worksheets

Vigil meditation

Box of vigil items

Forest Bathing

Provide a space outside where students can walk around within your line of site.

Lavender essential oil

Creativity spirituality (art)

Canvas

Art supplies

Creativity spirituality (movement)

Bluetooth speaker (or another device to play controlled music on)

Ribbon sticks

Creativity spirituality (written)

Lap desk for outdoor use

Notebook

Markers/crayons/colored pencils

Christian yoga meditation

Meditation music

Worksheet with yoga routine

Active listening meditation

Singing bowl

Active listening meditation worksheet

Self-reiki practice

All reiki worksheets

Gathering (30–45 min)

As students arrive have them pick up their floor mat and choose which form of spiritual self-care they connected with the most. Allow them thirty to forty-five minutes to sit in this space.

Opening (10 min)

At the conclusion of the allotted time, have students return to the center with their mats.

Opening Prayer (2 min)

"May we be blessed today by Your presence, Lord. May we understand more about Your Word and how we should conduct self-care. May You lift each of us up in You. Amen." (You can change the prayer to match your denomination or faith.)

The Lesson (30–40 min)

Provide each student with a worksheet and ask them to fill it out.

Once all students have completed the worksheet, they can choose to share what their plan is.

Positive Affirmation (2–5 min)

This is the only part of the class that is not challenge by choice. Every student must participate.

Have the students go around the room and say one positive thing about themselves. This can be anything from something they like about their appearance to something they are good at. Follow this statement by "and I love myself." They key is specificity. The comment cannot be generic.

Example: "I have beautiful eyes, and I love myself."

Closing (5–10 min)

Then pray: "Lord, thank you for bringing us all together today in this space. We pray for each person in this room and their mental health. May you guide them to a place of peace until we meet again."

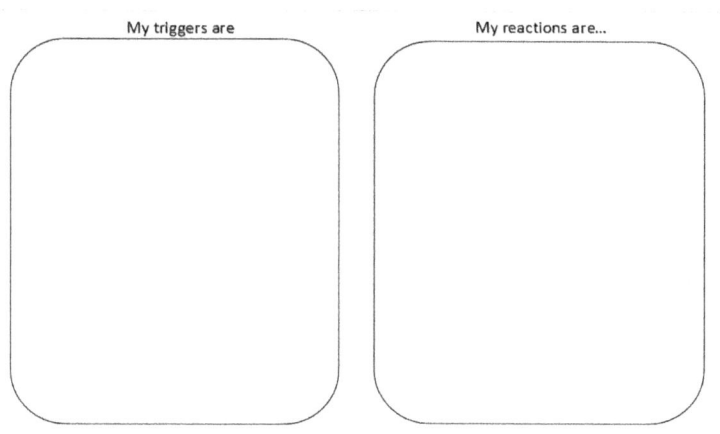

MY SPIRITUAL SELF-CARE PLAN

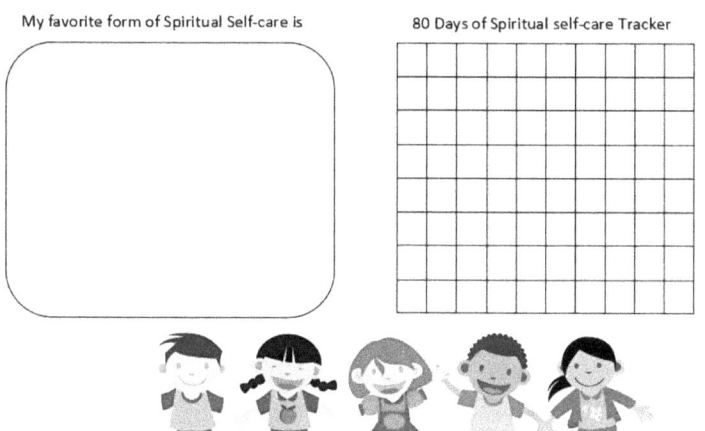

Bibliography

"3.3 National Suicide Prevention Strategy—Department of Health." Australian Government—Department of Health and Aged Care. https://www1.health.gov.au/internet/publications/publishing.nsf/Content/suicide-prevention-activities-evaluation~background~national-suicide-prevention-strategy.

"American Psychological Association Survey Shows Teen Stress Rivals That of Adults." American Psychological Association. https://www.apa.org/news/press/releases/2014/02/teen-stress.

"Anxiety, Depression, and Adolescent Suicide." Western Cape Government For You. Feb. 5, 2021. https://www.westerncape.gov.za/anxiety-depression-and-adolescent-suicide.

Arnautovska, Urška, and Onja T. Grad. "Attitudes Toward Suicide in the Adolescent Population." *Crisis* 31.1 (2010) 22–29.

Banstola, Ratna Shila, Tetsuya Ogino, and Sachiko Inoue. "Impact of Parents' Knowledge about the Development of Self-Esteem in Adolescents and Their Parenting Practice on the Self-Esteem and Suicidal Behavior of Urban High School Students in Nepal." *International Journal of Environmental Research and Public Health* 17.17 (2020) 6039.

Brewer, Rebecca, Richard Cook, and Geoffrey Bird. "Alexithymia: A General Deficit of Interoception." *Royal Society Open Science* 3.10 (2016) 150664.

Byrne, Michelle. "The Preliminary Outcomes of Mindfulness and Mental Health Interventions Across Deis and Non Deis Schools." PhD dissertation, Department of Psychology, DBS School of Arts, 2016.

Byrne, Michelle, and John Hyland. "The Preliminary Outcomes of Mindfulness and Mental Health Interventions Across Deis and Non Deis Schools." https://www.3ts.ie/docs/default-source/research/byrne2c-m.2c-2016-thesis.-preliminary-outcomes-of-mindfulness-and-mental-interventions.pdf?sfvrsn=e16188bd_5.

Bibliography

"Canadian Mental Health Association on Reconciliation and Mental Health." Canadian Mental Health Association. https://web.archive.org/web/20221025225903/https://cmha.ca/canadian-mental-health-association-on-reconciliation-and-mental-health/.

"C04.4: Teenage Suicides (15–19 years old)." OECD, Social Policy Division, Directorate of Employment, Labour and Social Affairs, 2017.

Cole-Lewis, Yasmin C., Polly Y. Gipson, Kiel J. Opperman, et al. "Protective Role of Religious Involvement Against Depression and Suicidal Ideation Among Youth with Interpersonal Problems." *Journal of Religious Health* 55.4 (2016) 1172–88.

Davis, D. M., and J. A. Hayes. "What Are the Benefits of Mindfulness? A Practice Review of Psychotherapy-Related Research." *Psychotherapy* 48.2 (2011) 198–208.

"Depression (Major Depressive Disorder)—Symptoms and Causes." Mayo Clinic. https://www.mayoclinic.org/diseases-conditions/depression/symptoms-causes/syc-20356007.

EveryMind, "Your Mental Wellness." https://everymind.org.au.

Fowler, James. *Stages of Faith: The Psychology of Human Development and the Quest for Meaning.* San Francisco: HarperOne, 1995.

Fuse, Toyomasa. "Suicide and Culture in Japan: A Study of Seppuku as an Institutionalized Form of Suicide." *Social Psychiatry* 15 (1980) 57–63.

Gini, Gianluca, and Dorothy L. Espelage. "Peer Victimization, Cyberbullying, and Suicide Risk in Children and Adolescents." *JAMA* 312.5 (2014) 545.

Goerlich, Katharina S. "The Multifaceted Nature of Alexithymia: A Neuroscientific Perspective." *Frontiers in Psychology* (2018) 1614.

Grimmond, Jessica, Rachel Kornhaber, Denis Visentin, and Michelle Cleary. "A Qualitative Systematic Review of Experiences and Perceptions of Youth Suicide." *PloS One* 14.6 (2019) 2–4.

Gutiérrez-Barroso, Josué, Fernando Barragán-Medero, and David Pérez-Jorge. "Suicide in Europe Countries: A Multivariate Approach Analysis." *Global Journal of Health Science* 10.4 (2018) 1–10.

Helbich, Marco, Paul L. Plener, Sebastian Hartung, et al. "Spatiotemporal Suicide Risk in Germany: A Longitudinal Study, 2007–11." *Scientific Reports* (2017) 7673.

"How Early Childhood Trauma Is Unique." Mar. 23, 2018. National Child Traumatic Stress Network. https://www.nctsn.org/what-is-child-trauma/trauma-types/early-childhood-trauma/effects.

Hunter, Rodney. *Dictionary of Pastoral Care and Counseling.* 3rd edition. New York: Abingdon, 2005.

"Ireland's National Strategy to Reduce Suicide, 2015–2020." Health Service Executive, Ireland. https://www.hse.ie/eng/services/list/4/mental-health-services/connecting-for-life/publications/connecting%20for%20life.pdf.

"Ireland's Teen Suicide Rate 4th Highest in EU/OECD." UNICEF. June 19, 2017. https://www.unicef.ie/2017/06/19/irelands-teen-suicide-rate-4th-highest-euoecd-unicef-report-card.

Bibliography

Jeon, Sun Y., Eric N. Reither, and Ryan K. Masters. "A Population-Based Analysis of Increasing Rates of Suicide Mortality in Japan and South Korea, 1985–2010." *BMC Public Health* 16 (2016) 356.

Kapusta, N. D., et al. "Rural-Urban Differences in Austrian Suicides." *Social Psychiatry and Psychiatric Epidemiology* 43 (2008) 311–18.

Kim, JaHun, Elaine Walsh, Kenneth Pike, et al. "Cyberbullying and Victimization and Youth Suicide Risk: The Buffering Effects of School Connectedness." *Journal of School Nursing* 36.4 (2019) 251–57.

Kinchin, Irina, and Christopher Doran. "The Cost of Youth Suicide in Australia." *International Journal of Environmental Research and Public Health* 15.4 (2018) 672.

King, Pamela, Linda Wagener Ebstyne, and Peter L. Benson. *The Handbook of Spiritual Development in Childhood and Adolescence*. Thousand Oaks, California: SAGE, 2005.

Kohlberg, Lawrence. *The Philosophy of Moral Development*. New York: Harper & Row, 1981.

Lasair, Simon. "What's the Point of Clinical Pastoral Education and Pastoral Counselling Education? Political, Developmental, and Professional Considerations." *Journal of Pastoral Care & Counseling* 74.1 (2020) 22–32.

Lee, Seung-yeon, Jun Sung Hong, and Dorothy L. Espelage. "An Ecological Understanding of Youth Suicide in South Korea." *School Psychology International* 31.5 (2010) 531–46.

Lesser, I. M. "A Review of the Alexithymia Concept." *Psychosomatic Medicine* 43.6 (1981) 531–43.

Liu, Li, Colin A. Capaldi, Heather M. Orpana, et al. "Changes over Time in Means of Suicide in Canada: An Analysis of Mortality Data from 1981 to 2018." *Canadian Medical Association Journal* 193.10 (2021) 331–38.

"Mental Health." Government of Ireland. https://www.gov.ie/en/policy-information/3aa528-mental-health/.

"Mental Health Service Learning Hub." Health Service Executive, Ireland. https://www.hse.ie/eng/services/list/4/mental-health-services.

Nagamitsu, Shinichiro, Masakazu Mimaki, Kenshi Koyanagi, et al. "Prevalence and Associated Factors of Suicidality in Japanese Adolescents: Results from a Population-Based Questionnaire Survey." *BMC Pediatrics* 20.1 (2020) 467.

Naito, Ayumi. "Internet Suicide in Japan: Implications for Child and Adolescent Mental Health." *Clinical Child Psychology and Psychiatry* 12.4 (2007) 583–97.

Nastasi, Bonnie Kaul, Stuart N. Hart, and Shereen C Naser. *International Handbook on Child Rights and School Psychology*. Cham, Switzerland: Springer, 2020.

The Nippon Foundation. "The Nippon Foundation Suicide Prevention Project." 2016. https://www.nippon-foundation.or.jp/en/what/projects/suicide-measures.

Bibliography

O'Connor, Rory C., and Olivia J. Kirtley. "The Integrated Motivational-Volitional Model of Suicidal Behaviour." *Philosophical Transactions of the Royal Society of London, Series B, Biological Sciences* 373.1754 (2018) 1–10.

O'Connor, Rory C., and Matthew K Nock. "The Psychology of Suicidal Behaviour." *Lancet Psychiatry* 1.1 (Jun. 2014) 73–85.

O'Donnell, Meaghan L., James A. Agathos, Olivia Metcalf, et al. "Adjustment Disorder: Current Developments and Future Directions." *International Journal of Environmental Research and Public Health* (2019) 2537.

Olson, Robert. "Suicide and Stigma." Centre for Suicide Prevention. https://www.suicideinfo.ca/resource/suicideandstigma/.

"The Origin of Forest Bathing and Forest Therapy." Nature Connection World. https://community.natureconnection.world.

Piaget, Jean, et al. *The Psychology of the Child*. New York: Basic Books, 1972.

"Preventing Suicide: A Global Imperative." World Health Organization. https://web.archive.org/web/20200307145148/https://www.who.int/mental_health/suicide-prevention/world_report_2014/en/.

Roehlkepartain, Eugene C., Pamela King, Linda Wagener, et al. *The Handbook of Spiritual Development in Childhood and Adolescence*. Thousand Oaks, CA: Sage, 2006.

Russell, Roxanne, Daniel Metraux, and Mauricio Tohen. "Cultural Influences on Suicide in Japan." *Psychiatry and Clinical Neurosciences* 71.1 (2017) 2–5.

Schlebusch, L. "Suicide Prevention: A Proposed National Strategy for South Africa." *African Journal of Psychiatry* 15.6 (2012) 5.

Skinner, Robin, Steven McFaull, Anne E. Rhodes, et al. "Suicide in Canada." *Canadian Journal of Psychiatry* 61.7 (2016) 405–12.

Stricka, Marius, and Marija Jakubauskiene. "Suicide Prevention: A Case of Lithuania." *European Journal of Public Health* 26(suppl 1) (Nov. 2016) 188.

Sharp, Sonia. "How Much Does Bullying Hurt? The Effects of Bullying on the Personal Wellbeing and Educational Progress of Secondary Aged Students." *Educational and Child Psychology* (1995) 81–88

Shirakawa, Osamu. "Do Cultural Factors Still Exert an Impact on the Suicide Rate in Japan?" *Psychiatry and Clinical Neurosciences* 71.1 (2017) 1.

Slander, Dawn. "Rainbow Meditation Script." https://www.dawnselander.com/wp-content/uploads/2019/04/Rainbow-Meditation.pdf.

"Stress in America: Generation Z." American Psychological Association. https://www.apa.org/news/press/releases/stress/2018/stress-gen-z.pdf.

"Suicide." World Health Organization (WHO). https://www.who.int/news-room/fact-sheets/detail/suicide.

"Suicide & Self-Harm Monitoring." Australian Institute of Health and Welfare. https://www.aihw.gov.au/suicide-self-harm-monitoring.

"Suicide in Canada: Key Statistics." Government of Canada. https://www.canada.ca/en/public-health/services/publications/healthy-living/suicide-canada-key-statistics-infographic.html.

"Suicide in Ireland Survey." https://web.archive.org/web/20211229032945/https://www.3ts.ie/research-support/research/all-ireland-suicide-survey/.

Bibliography

"Suicide Prevention." World Health Organization (WHO). https://web.archive.org/web/20240308050725/https://www.who.int/health-topics/suicide.

"Suicide Prevention in Europe." World Health Organization (WHO). https://iris.who.int/bitstream/handle/10665/107452/E77922.pdf;sequence=1.

"Suicide Prevention in Japan: A Public Health Priority." https://www.who.int/news-room/feature-stories/detail/suicide-prevention-in-japan--a-public-health-priority.

"Suicide Prevention Programs." Everymind. https://everymind.org.au/programs/suicide-prevention-programs.

Tsukahara, Teruomi, Hiroaki Arai, Tomoko Kamijo, et al. "The Relationship Between Attitudes Toward Suicide and Family History of Suicide in Nagano Prefecture, Japan." *International Journal of Environmental Research and Public Health* 13.6 (2016) 623.

Turecki G, Brent DA. "Suicide and Suicidal Behaviour." *Lancet* 387 (Mar 19, 2016) 1227–39.

"Understanding Suicide, Suicide Attempts and Self-Harm in Primary School Aged Children." Headspace. https://headspace.org.au/assets/download-cards/02-HSP254-Suicide-in-Primary-Schools-Summary-FA-low-res2.pdf.

Wasserman, Danuta. "Review of Health and Risk-Behaviours, Mental Health Problems and Suicidal Behaviours in Young Europeans on the Basis of the Results from the EU-Funded Saving and Empowering Young Lives in Europe (SEYLE) Study." *Psychiatria Polska* 50.6 (2016) 1093–1107.

"World Health Report: 2002." World Health Organization (WHO). https://www.who.int/publications/i/item/9241562072

Yonemoto, Naohiro, Yoshitaka Kawashima, Kaori Endo, et al. "Implementation of Gatekeeper Training Programs for Suicide Prevention in Japan: A Systematic Review." *International Journal of Mental Health Systems* 13.1 (2019) 2.

Yoshioka, E., S. Hanley, Y. Kawanishi, et al. "Time Trends in Method-Specific Suicide Rates in Japan, 1990–2011." *Epidemiology and Psychiatric Sciences* 25.1 (2016) 58–68.

www.ingramcontent.com/pod-product-compliance
Lightning Source LLC
Chambersburg PA
CBHW072134160426
43197CB00012B/2103